THE PSYCHIC AND THE SPIRITUAL

THE PSYCHIC AND THE SPIRITUAL

WHAT IS THE DIFFERENCE?

by

JOHN WHITE

www.whitecrowbooks.com

CONTENTS

INTRODUCTION

An ancient insight about higher human development states very simply: 'Psychic development is not the same as spiritual growth.' In the course of one's spiritual growth, i.e., actualizing your potential for higher human development, there are dangers, dead-ends, byways and traps of which to beware. A principal source of such difficulties is the failure to distinguish between the psychic and the spiritual. All sacred traditions recognize this. They have made explicit warnings about it and have formulated doctrinal statements and instructional practices to guide people safely along the path to enlightenment and God-realization.

There is a hierarchical relation between the two and spiritual growth is senior, higher. I have known many powerful psychics and have personally experienced their abilities, but those abilities haven't done much for their character development, which in some cases was sadly immature. If the name of the game is enlightenment, pursuing psychic powers can be a waste of time, a dead end. If psychic abilities develop along the way in the context of spiritual unfoldment, fine, but don't mistake them for enlightenment.

Psychic abilities often spontaneously manifest themselves in the course of spiritual unfoldment and are there in people waiting to be cultivated. But always the question is, cultivated to what end? Evidence abounds in the history of psychical research and its successor, parapsychology, to show that renowned psychics were often deficient in one or more character traits which are universally regarded as necessary for spiritual growth. Conceit and vanity about one's psychic abilities are incompatible with God-realization. So are dishonesty and a desire to dominate people. These undesirable qualities, and others, have been seen to one degree or another in some "superpsychics" whose egotism has led them to behave in decidedly unspiritual ways. Accounts of possible fraud and trickery are not hard to find in connection with both famous and lesser-known psychics; their base motives—to be rich, famous, powerful, to control and use others for personal gain, and so forth—are totally contrary to spiritual living.

One of the best-known American mediums, the Rev. Arthur Ford, inspired the founding of Spiritual Frontiers Fellowship (SFF) partly to address this problem. SFF is now defunct, but its goals were the development of spiritual growth in the individual and encouragement of new dimensions of spiritual experience within the institutional churches. Ford was keenly aware of the problem of misused psychic and spiritual gifts, and stated flatly in his biography, *Unknown But Known*, that being psychic did not at all make one spiritual.

This lesson—the psychic is not the spiritual—has been given major emphasis in the teaching of all the world's major spiritual and religious traditions. Yogic philosophy warns against seeking *siddhis* (psychic powers) because they can be obstacles to enlightenment. St. Paul spoke at length on this same subject, using different terminology, in chapters 12 to 24 of his Letter to the Corinthians. While plainly acknowledging that people have a "spiritual body" separable from the physical body and that there are "diversities of gifts" such as clairvoyance, prophecy, healing, mediumship, and so forth, he emphasized that, without a solid moral foundation in one's character, such abilities are "as sounding brass or a tinkling cymbal." His discourse on love as the essential element in one's thought and behavior has relevance to all who are interested in psychic development.

Even occult traditions, such as witchcraft, note the difference between the "left hand" or evil path of black magic and the "right hand," or benevolent path of white magic, and emphasize that evil worked on someone will eventually boomerang upon the black magician. The legend of the sorcerer's apprentice is a powerful example. The ancient German tale, given widespread notice through its modern presentation in Walt Disney's *Fantasia*, teaches very explicitly: paranormal powers can get out of hand and harm the psychic himself, as well as others, unless there is a sound emotional, moral and intellectual basis from which the psychic applies his powers.

The same lesson is found in Tibetan Buddhism in the legend of its most famous saint, Milarepa. As a young man, Milarepa studied sorcery, attaining great powers. But he used them to create pain and suffering upon his family and villagers, who drove him out. In remorse for his evil actions, he studied yoga, eventually becoming a great yogi. Even in his old age, however, Milarepa lamented his harmful—and shameful—misuse of his psychic abilities.

The modern world has its own warnings of the same danger, and it is given most forcefully in the popular culture media of comic books and movies. Since the first editions of *Superman, Batman* and *Captain Marvel,* superheroes with extraordinary abilities such as x-ray vision, superhearing, superstrength, and imperviousness to bullets, fire and pain have been there to tempt their possessors to misuse them. But the superheroes do not succumb to the temptation. However, their evil opponents, who sometimes have the same superpowers, do misuse them, and the story line always powerfully underscores the evil of such actions.

We see the same thing on screen with the superhero movies. Most notable are the recent *X-Men* films, where Wolverine and his fellow mutants have superhuman abilities and superpsychic talents, but always the abilities and talents are used for good to oppose other mutant humans with similar capabilities who lack the moral and ethical safeguards against misusing them.

In short, the benevolent use of psychic functioning requires a high degree of character development and a balanced, integrated personality—indispensable aspects of spiritual unfoldment and God-realization. Without them, the psychic person can get into difficulties which cannot be handled easily or wisely. These difficulties may include delusional belief, uncontrolled telepathy (hearing voices), poltergeist manifestations unleashed by psychokinetic forces, possession by nonphysical entities (giving rise to multiple personality disorders), and a conceited pride or megalomania in which the psychic assumes the position of infallibility and ultimate authority over others.

The following chapters can help you to become more sensitive to the spiritual realm, to distinguish it from the psychic realm, and to be more knowledgeable about both. They also offer what I think are sensible, prudent cautions which ought to be taken by those who seek psychic development. In that regard, it is wise to bear in mind Jesus' injunction: "Seek ye first the Kingdom of God and his righteousness; and all these things shall be added unto you." (Matthew 6:33, KJV)

This Introduction originally appeared as my introduction to a collection of articles by other writers entitled *The Psychic and the Spiritual:*

What's the Difference? I produced it for the Spiritual Frontiers Fellowship in 1986. I chose the title and have retained it for this book. I have edited and expanded my introduction somewhat, and I use it here because it still serves as a useful entry point to my own collected essays and articles on this theme—produced over three decades—which I present here. The material begins with a look at the purely psychic, but proceeds to higher levels of understanding in which the spiritual is presented with increasing clarity and comprehensiveness, and is distinguished from the psychic, and always in the context of transcending the ego for the sake of enlightenment.

PART 1

UNDERSTANDING THE PSYCHIC

CHAPTER I

SUPERPSYCHIC

A REPORT ON URI GELLER

T he scientific controversy surrounding the Israeli psychic Uri Geller reached epic proportions shortly after he came to the United States in 1972. He was praised and damned in the press, scientific literature and a handful of books about him. For every supporter (such as science writer Arthur C. Clarke who witnessed several mind-boggling events and then challenged Geller's critics to put up or shut up) there has been a detractor (such as, James "The Amazing" Randi, a professional magician who claims that everything Geller does is merely sleight-of-hand and illusion). This article appeared in *Psychic Observer/Chimes*, Vol. 36, No. 1, January-March 1975. I have expanded it with additional observations of Geller's psychic abilities.

In *New Scientist's* report on the Israeli psychic Uri Geller (October 17, 1974) by Joe Hanlon, I am portrayed as a "naive" believer. Now, I don't claim to be a scientist or even scientifically trained, although I have had a fair amount of such training while earning a degree at Dartmouth College, which I attended on an NROTC scholarship. My naval science training, in parallel with my normal college studies, was later augmented by various naval school technical courses while on active duty, including Nuclear Weapons School. In addition, I have been "briefed" by a professional magician on means of duplicating the key-bending for which Geller is famous.

Furthermore, I acknowledge that while a person is entitled to be wrong in his opinions, it is inexcusable to be wrong in his facts. But for me, belief can be rational or irrational. Rational belief—faith, if you will—grows out of personal experience and observations tested by reason and, insofar as possible, scientific validation. Thus I would characterize my belief in Geller's paranormal abilities as rationally based on facts, logic and sound analysis.

My interest is in knowing the truth as fully as I can perceive it, and I remain open to definitive proof that Geller "augments" his performances if he cannot deliver a genuine psychic event. But the widely made inference that Geller cheats, based on the article in *Popular Photography* (June 1974) which "exposed" him, is unjustified. Nowhere did the authors say Geller cheated. They only said they could duplicate Geller's results by removing the lens cap. (Geller had caused photographic images to appear on unexposed film.) Dr. Andrija Puharich, Geller's mentor at the time, told me that he was present during the entire session and there was no cheating.

But even if there were, 99 instances of deception do not disprove one genuine event, and Geller has a much higher batting average for producing paranormal events than that. The question is not whether Geller's effects can be duplicated by stage magic, slight of hand, illusion or sophisticated technology; many can. The real question is whether Geller does, in fact, use such means. It would not surprise me to find out that he does because the history of psychic research is rife with such occurrences, but my observations of Geller thus far indicate he is indeed a superpsychic. As William James, the Harvard psychologist who was a founder of the American Society for Psychical Research in 1884, said, "It only takes one white crow to prove not all crows are black."

Therefore I would like to inform readers of four "simple immediate" demonstrations of the sort Hanlon was seeking in his investigations—the kind which provide a basis for my rational belief.

But first, some background for readers.

I first met Geller at the home of Dr. Andrija Puharich, M.D., in Ossining, New York in April 1972. Puharich was a long-time investigator in psychic phenomena and had been researching Geller closely for about a year. I was working for Apollo 14 astronaut, Dr. Edgar Mitchell, who became the sixth man on the moon in February 1971 during his lunar voyage. While going to and from the moon, Mitchell conducted a telepathy experiment which made world headlines. Shortly thereafter, he retired from the Navy and founded the Institute of Noetic Sciences (IONS) in Menlo Park, California, to study the powers of the human mind. I was his Director of Education. Also present at Puharich's home were Dr. Gerald Feinberg of the Physics Department of Columbia University in New York City, Dr. Wilbur Franklin (mentioned in Hanlon's article) of Kent State University's Physics Department, and half a dozen other guests.

Puharich had brought Geller to Mitchell's attention as a research subject. Israeli-born Geller claimed to have discovered early in life that he had psychic powers. At age seven, he found he could move the hands of a watch psychokinetically just by "wishing" it was later in the day. But Geller didn't begin his public demonstrations of his amazing abilities until his early twenties, after he served as a paratrooper in the Israeli army and, later, as a photographer's model. These demonstrations usually took the form of a night club performance. Among Israeli parapsychologists, this brought him an unfavorable reputation.

Puharich thought otherwise, however. He had gone to Israel in 1971 to investigate rumors of a real "man of miracles." Puharich was a veteran investigator of the paranormal and occult. He had been into things on the psychic research frontier long before they became public knowledge. Having "been around," he wasn't likely to be fooled. As it turned out, he was soon convinced—indeed, overwhelmed. Geller demonstrated many kinds of paranormal phenomena such as bending metal objects without touching them and even dematerializing them.

So in April 1972, Mitchell and I went to Puharich's home to meet and observe Geller. Mitchell had raised funds to bring Geller to America so scientific testing under controlled conditions could be performed. That would be done shortly thereafter at Stanford Research Institute (or SRI as it was known) in Menlo Park, California, near the offices of IONS.

An Interesting Day

That was a very interesting day. The first thing Geller did was cut through a specially machined 14-carat gold ring provided by Franklin and twist it into an S-shape—without touching it. When I tried to bend it back, I found out how strong 14-carat gold is. I couldn't budge it!

Next, Geller took Mitchell's astronaut watch, which is a complex instrument with four hands and two stems for moving them, and set the watch face down on a coffee table. Then, holding his hand over the watch but not touching it, he concentrated on moving the hands. When it was turned over, the hands had moved ahead one hour and eight minutes.

Then came two of the "simple, immediate" demonstrations Hanlon calls for.

At Geller's request for objects to work with, one of the women produced a large steel safety pin—the size used for baby cloth diapers—and some other items, including a common metal straight pin. The woman was a neighbor of Dr. Puharich who claimed to have met Geller for the first time that day; the items were contained in her purse.

I opened the safety pin and held it at the circular base, observing that it was not deformed in any way and that it was indeed an ordinary metal safety pin. (As father of four children, I had plenty of experience with diapers and diaper pins.) Then, while I held it and the others were watching, Geller lightly stroked the pointed half in the middle between his thumb and forefinger. If there had been the slightest pressure from muscular effort by Geller, I would have felt it. But there was no such pressure. I estimate that he rubbed the pin for no more than 15 seconds.

Even as Geller was stroking the pin, we could see it begin to bend outward (toward him) between his fingers. When that happened, he removed his hand from the pin. We could see it continuing to bend in my hand. After a minute or so, I placed it on a saucer in the middle of the dinner table around which we had gathered. During the next five minutes, the pin deformed still further, eventually bending in the middle of the pointed half about 30 degrees from the original position until it looked like a square root sign. During that time no one touched the pin.

The second event took place shortly afterward while we were eating. After bending the pin, Geller felt he had exhausted his psychic ability for the time being, so we sat down to lunch and began talking. I sat two places to Geller's right, with a woman between us. Geller and the woman began talking, and I listened. The straight pin which had been produced earlier by the neighbor was also lying on the saucer in the middle of the table.

Suddenly there was a loud, sharp sound, like a child's cap gun firing, and the straight pin exploded in half. The halves flew off the dish across the table in opposite directions. At that precise moment I was observing Geller, so I can attest that he did not physically touch the pin.

The pointed end shot across the table in Geller's direction and fell to the floor. The other half remained on the table, landing in front of Feinberg. Geller immediately knew what had happened, but was even more excited about it than the rest of us because, he said, he hadn't done it or at least hadn't mean to. His position was: it just happened, that's all, and I don't know why.

When we recovered the halves of the pin and examined them, there seemed to be an unusual surface at the point of parting. A smooth surface was evident, cleanly dividing the pin at an angle perpendicular to the long axis. No striation was noticeable.

Puharich produced a pair of wire cutters at Feinberg's request, and Feinberg then cut through one half of the pin to compare the cleavage pattern with the original. The difference was readily seen, since the original showed no signs of deformation due to bending or cutting. Franklin later had the pin analyzed, and the cleavage pattern at the tip of each half was found to be perfectly smooth and slightly rounded. Moreover, Franklin found that material was missing from the tips of each half—precisely the amount which would have restored each half to its original regular shape. Such an effect cannot be produced by any known means under those circumstances unless one supposes that the woman who produced the pin was an accomplice and that Geller had prepared it ahead of time in a way which implies he has access to technology almost as superior as his presumed paranormal abilities.

Stanford Research Institute

It was these events and others of a similarly impressive nature witnessed there which persuaded Mitchell to proceed with fundraising to underwrite the cost of the experiments at SRI. The events of the day were more than adequate to convince him that Geller was genuine. He moved quickly to raise money and arrange for scientists to test Geller. Two recent acquaintances of his got the nod: Dr. Harold Puthoff and Russell Targ, research scientists at SRI. Several months later Geller was tested by them at the giant brain factory, and in due time their report was published in the august British scientific journal, *Nature*, where it stirred up an international hornets nest.

I'll give two more examples of Geller's paranormal abilities. One was recorded in 1973 on Super-8 color movie film by James Bolen, editor and publisher of *Psychic* magazine in San Francisco. Frames from it were shown in the June 1973 issue. The frames clearly show the breaking apart—not simply bending—of a fork which Bolen had personally verified as being intact before the demonstration. Bolen described the event this way:

> Uri was moving his left thumb and index finger over the middle part of the fork as I was filming him. He then said the metal was becoming soft and that it was beginning to bend. I zoomed in on his hands and the fork. I asked him to open his fingers to reveal the area. As he did, the prong part began falling apart slowly, as though the metal had become plastic where he had held it. It then came completely apart, with the prong part falling down, but as it fell it drew away a short threadlike piece of metal. I examined both pieces of the fork at the break which looked as though it had melted apart. Uri did not seem to feel any heat.

The articles editor of *Psychic* magazine, Alan Vaughan, also observed Geller's psychokinetic ability. In the same issue he reported:

> Before the SRI physicists gave their scientific report on Geller before a physics colloquium in Columbia University in New York, *Time* magazine had already branded Geller a magician, later saying that he has a 'highly questionable record.' *Time* intimated that a magician could easily duplicate all of Geller's feats, even the bending of metals by touching them lightly. So I proposed to Bolen the following experimental idea: Let Geller bend an object that is held in my hands and which he does not touch. If he can do that I will have to give up my skepticism. When Geller visited San Francisco to be interviewed by *Psychic*, he was able to do just that. Taking a hotel room key, Bolen first attempted to bend it by manual means. He succeeded only in raising a blood blister. He handed the key to Geller who, holding it by the handle, handed it to me. I grasped the key by the large end and put my other hand on top. Geller put his hand lightly on top of mine. He asked me if my hands felt any sensation, but they did not. Then he asked me to look at it. It was bent 30 degrees and was still slightly bending as I watched. The whole procedure was witnessed by Bolen.

Hanlon points out that our perceptions are closely wedded to our conceptions. But he points this out for only one side of the question. Events such as these, I maintain, cannot be explained as due to normal—albeit fraudulent—means. Rather, events such as these will continue to require examinations by scientists who are "open-minded" but do not have a "hole in the head." Let them be skeptical, but not presume the impossibility of certain events since the "sheep-goat effect" which psychic research recognizes can influence the outcome of an experiment, depending on the mind-set, either positive or negative, of both the experiment and the subject. And let them realize more generally how preconceptions and nonconscious assumptions, i.e., the paradigm from which they observe events, can mediate perception so that they do not see to the same degree that Hanlon's "believers" see.

The film *Field of Dreams* portrays such a situation. In it, a man who does not share the hero's paradigm or conception of reality, which includes seeing the spirits of deceased baseball players playing baseball in an Iowa cornfield ball park, walks onto the field in front of home plate, oblivious to it all and narrowly avoids being hit by an unseen pitched ball. The scene humorously illustrates the reverse of the saying, "I'll believe it when I see it." Rather, from the point of view of the film, what's true is "I'll see it when I believe it." The man does finally see the ball players, but only after he has a deep psychological shift of mind.

Finally, let skeptical scientists be aware of the fact that science can study only what its methodology allows it to study and that it leaves out those aspects of human experience and behavior which are not amenable to its method. (This, incidentally, is why Dr. J. B. Rhine, the "father" of parapsychology, chose to forego extended investigation of the life-after-death hypothesis when he began his work in the 1930s. It did not mean he didn't "believe" in post-mortem existence; in fact, he did. It meant only that the subject was, in his opinion, beyond the reach of scientific investigation at the time.)

Another Superpsychic

Another personal experience of mine is pertinent here. In 1975, while attending a conference in Chicago, I had lunch with the well-known psychic Olof Jonsson, who was one of the four "receivers" on Earth to whom Mitchell telepathically sent images during his ESP experiment aboard the Apollo 14 lunar voyage. (Jonsson is now deceased.) During our meal, with several other people at the table, Jonsson demonstrated his telepathic ability. He took out a deck of ordinary playing cards which he habitually carried with him. The pattern on the back of the cards consisted of small white dots against a black background. Jonsson then told me he would mentally project an image to me. He drew the image on a piece of paper, allowing no one to see it. Then he folded it and put it aside. Next he told me to look at the back of a card laying on the table before me. As I did, some of the white dots appeared to change color and became a glowing yellow-gold. The only dots to do so were the ones needed to form a perfect star about one inch wide which stood out brilliantly against the black background.

Jonsson then asked me what I had seen. "I saw a star," I told him, describing what had occurred in my perception. Then he unfolded the paper and showed everyone the star he had drawn. It was a perfect match. No one else had seen any change in the color of the dots, however, so it was perfectly obvious that I had experienced a minor but very real visual hallucination triggered by Jonsson's telepathic transmission. (Hallucination is defined as perception of something without a physical referent.)

Similarly, Mitchell experienced the telepathic reception of an image that day in 1972 when we first met Geller. He told Mitchell to look across the room at the white wall, where he would see an image appear which Geller would transmit. Geller then sketched on a piece of paper the image he was going to telepathically send to Mitchell, and held it in his hand until he had completed the transmission. As Mitchell gazed at the wall, he saw the same thing happen which I did several years later with Jonsson. An image constructed from brilliant light appeared on the wall to Mitchell's gaze—an image which no one else in the room saw. Mitchell then described what he had seen, after which Geller verified it by showing the paper with the same image on it.

Here's another anecdote to show Geller's genuine psychic ability. At the very beginning of that day at Puharich's home, Geller went outside and picked a green bud from shrubbery near the front door. He came back inside, showed a few of us the green bud, and said he would make it change color. The bud was laying in the palm of his hand; we could see it clearly and examined it. Then he closed his hand into a fist and concentrated. Perhaps thirty seconds later, he opened his hand. The green bud had withered into a brown and obviously dead condition.

The Joe Hanlons of the world will immediately object that Geller had used sleight of hand to deceive us. I'm sure he didn't, but let that criticism stand for the moment while I describe another such incident.

About a decade later, I went to a reception in New York City where Geller was present. As a demonstration, he took out a sealed commercial packet of radish seeds, tore it open, and sprinkled a few seeds into his hand. As he'd done with the green bud at Puharich's home, he simply held his hand open, palm up, so all could see the seeds. They were brown and in the condition which radish seeds have in their packet when for sale.

Next Geller closed his hand. His other hand never went near the open palm with the seeds. So when he closed his hand, we all were certain the seeds were there and in the condition we'd just seen. Again, he held his hand closed for perhaps thirty seconds. Then he opened it. The same seeds were there, but several of them had begun to sprout. A root was visible coming out of them. The largest root was about one-eighth of an inch long and had the greenish-white color of a sprout just emerging from its husk. The energy which Geller worked with to blight a green bud was now used in reverse to initiate growth of the radish seeds. It was impressive.

Geller may be "a good magician," but he is also clearly a superpsychic. He is gifted with paranormal powers which *true* magicians have used for millennia—powers such as telepathy, clairvoyance and psychokinesis. After Puharich publishes the research reports he has collected from independent investigators, this should be clear. [The reports appeared as a book entitled *The Geller Papers: Scientific Observations on the Paranormal Powers of Uri Geller*, edited by Charles Panati and published by Houghton-Mifflin in 1976. It contained the actual scientific reports written by researchers who have studied Geller under controlled conditions in more than a dozen laboratories around the world. In those situations, he performed psychic feats which clearly are beyond the ability of stage magicians to duplicate.]

Diehard skeptics such as Randi will never accept that Geller is a real psychic. But for open, inquiring minds, the question is: How does he do it?

Meanwhile, readers should be aware that Geller is not the only superpsychic around. Verbal reports from reputable sources are circulating in the psychic research community to the effect that other superpsychics, some surpassing Geller, are now being investigated. On this basis, I suggest that the question of Uri Geller and science is far from settled by Hanlon's investigation.

CHAPTER 2

ON MIND AND THE PHYSICS OF PARANORMAL PHENOMENA

M y 1977 anthology *Future Science: Life Energies and the Physics of Paranormal Phenomena* is divided into several parts, each with an introduction by me. This chapter is an expansion of a lecture I developed from the introductory material.

The Occult Forces of Life

The reigning world view of the scientific community or, to use more current jargon, the consensual reality, has been described as materialistic, reductionistic and atheistic. As a formal philosophy which attempts to give *meaning* to its data, it has been called physicalism. The term denotes a widespread assumption in science, which has been present from its beginning, that the secret of life is inherent in the properties of matter.

From the viewpoint of physicalism, life itself is the ultimate paranormal event. The universe is assumed to consist only of physical matter. It has no "spirit," no principle of vitality beyond the physical. In short, it has no metaphysics. The four basic forces which modern science recognizes—electromagnetism, gravity, the weak and strong nuclear forces—are assumed to arise from properties of physical matter, albeit in its subtlest form. All phenomena, this philosophy says, including life and mental activity, will finally be reduced to an explanation in terms of these energies and physicochemical mechanisms acting in random fashion without purpose, meaning or direction from any higher intelligence. If only we can get a fine enough analysis (the physicalist line of thinking goes), if only we can combine chemicals in the right way with the right amount of electricity, we can create life.

Mind is the hallmark of life and should therefore, from the physicalist point of view, be inherent in the properties of matter. But it isn't, as I showed in "Neuroscience and the New View of Mind." If mind is not to be found in the recognized forces of nature, we will have to look for it elsewhere.

Parapsychology and psychical research are doing precisely that. A century and a half of investigation into paranormal phenomena has established a wide range of events which clearly are *real* events. But what is the energy involved in these events? How can it be controlled and directed? What can we say with certainty and precision about the physics of these events?

The word energy comes from the Greek *energeia*, meaning "active." It is generally understood as the capacity to do work or to be active. But in its original sense it means *vital* activity, that which can move or quicken inert matter. En-erg-y means literally "of (itself) motivational-ness."

Thus, in earlier times, for many people there was a distinct and publicly acknowledged sense of a fundamental life force. This life force was self-evident to the ancients, even though its nature was not readily understood. It was apprehended but not fully comprehended—recognized but not well explained. It was normally undetected, secret, hidden from sensory processes and from rational understanding. It was, in a word, occult.

In recent years, an increasing number of investigators seeking to understand paranormal phenomena have come to feel that science must recognize a new principle in nature—the same principle of vitality or livingness which ancient traditions considered primary. This principle introduces what may be called a *psychic* factor, coming from *psyche*, meaning "soul" or "mind." And thus there has been a reawakening of interest in those ancient traditions which claim to have knowledge of the creative life force—what could be called a fifth force.

One researcher, electrical engineer Lawrence Beynam of Ankara, Turkey, summarized his views on the subject by saying there is an energy in living organisms which is weak and unpredictable, but it can be refracted, polarized, focussed and combined with other energies. It sometimes has effects similar to magnetism, electricity, heat and luminous radiation, but it is none of these. Attempts to control and employ the energy have met with little success; investigators have not yet defined the laws governing its operation.

Addressing himself to the same topic, the fortean-naturalist Ivan Sanderson, founder of the Society to Investigate the Unexplained, editorialized in the society's journal *Pursuit* on the nature of the "new" force:

This fifth force is certainly involved in various aspects of SSP [supersensory proclivities, his term for psychic abilities] and it would now seem to be the major force operative in the true psychic field and possibly the only one acting therein. Its manifestations are in no way affected by any of the other known forces; and, while doubtless universal in nature, it can be observed, measured and investigated only in the biological field. The presence of a living thing is necessary to bring it to light. Although we have not yet defined it or its parameters, it has now been demonstrated that it, and it alone, can explain a whole raft of what were previously thought to be mysteries or pure imagination, such as mental telepathy, SSP [here meaning supersensory projection] and SSR [supersensory reception], the two PKs—psychokinesis and pyrokinesis—and possibly the whole group of things clustering around clairvoyance. It would explain all that has puzzled the psychologists about things like the so-called subconscious, hypnotism, and the like.[1]

Sanderson pointed out that psychics such as Peter Hurkos, who once demonstrated telepathy while inside a Faraday cage (see Andrija Puharich's *Beyond Telepathy* for an account of this), show that these abilities do not function along electromagnetic lines. Uri Geller's performance of the same feat, reported by Stanford Research Institute scientists Harold Puthoff and Russell Targ in *Nature* (October 1974) reconfirms the phenomenon. Experiments in the Soviet Union by Leonid Vasiliev in the 1930's also indicated this hypothesized fifth force.

"Is it not time," Sanderson asked in his editorial, "that we stopped ignoring all these things, or blithely relegating them to that vague field of the psychic, and got the technicians to work, trying to define the nature of this force and, by both theory and experimentation, give us a set of laws for it such as govern the other four forces?" He pointed out that there is ample published material to begin with, so that a "basic pattern" might be assembled almost immediately. "There is then," he concluded, "the matter of seeking its parameters and fitting new observations into this pattern, rejecting them, or altering the pattern."

As I pointed out in *Future Science*, this fundamental force seems to have been recognized many times in history by various prescientific traditions. Appendix 1 to it shows that accounts of a mysterious energy run through ancient occult and spiritual documents. For example, the 18th century French magus, Eliphas Levi, in his book *Transcendental Magic*, described the properties of the magician's "astral light" this way: "there exists an agent which is natural and divine, material and spiritual, a universal plastic mediator, a common receptacle of the vibrations of motion and the images of form, a fluid and a force, which may be called in some way the Imagination of Nature... The existence of this force is the great Arcanum of practical Magic."

More than 100 other names for this mysterious energy have been identified from various sources around the world. In the Orient, for example, the Chinese conception of *qi* or *chi* (*ki* in Japanese) was thought to be the intrinsic vital force throughout all creation. It is this life energy which acupuncture manipulates to maintain health and which can be concentrated through disciplines such as tai chi and aikido to perform paranormal acts. According to Confucianism and Taoism, without qi, nothing can exist, and from it spring the yin and yang forces which in turn give rise to all things, including living organisms.

Paralleling this idea in the yogic tradition of India and Tibet is the notion of *prana*. The same concept can be found in practically every culture. Polynesians and Hawaiians call it *mana*. To the Sufis, it is *baraka*. It is *yesod* in the Jewish cabalistic tradition. The Iroquois call it *orenda*; the Ituri pygmies, *megbe*. In Christianity, it is the Holy Spirit (see "The Paranormal in Judeo-Christianity" in my *The Meeting of Science and Spirit*). These and many other traditions claim to recognize and, in some cases, control a vital cosmic energy underlying paranormal phenomena.

Within modern times there have also been people who claim to have identified *through science* a fifth and fundamental force in nature. Wilhelm Reich is perhaps the most notable figure. His discovery of *orgone* energy is considered by orgonomists to be at the heart of science and life itself. In the Reichian view, orgone is the all-pervasive ocean of life energy—primordial, massless and pre-atomic—from which all other forms of energy are derived. Some investigators see parallels between it and both Franz Anton Mesmer's *animal magnetism* and Karl von

Reichenbach's *odic force.* There is a parallel, too, between it and the Soviet concept of biplasma.

There are many traditions, both ancient and contemporary, which claim to have identified the energy behind paranormal phenomena. I collected them in *Future Science* and called them "X-energy." In listing them, I felt it best to be all-inclusive rather than selective, yet it was apparent that the terms are not fully synonymous in all cases. There are varying measures of overlap or convergence among some of them. Prana, for example, is said by yogic tradition to have a number of gradations. Likewise, there are various forms of chi. Rudolf Steiner's presentation of the etheric formative forces lists seven—the life ether, the chemical ether, the light ether, the warmth ether and three "higher" ethers. The chemical ether seems equivalent to orgone. Orgone itself, however, is single-state. In general, however, the terms I noted as forms of X-energy point toward the idea of a new principle in nature for science to recognize in the form of a metaphysical or spiritual, but nonetheless real, creative life force.

As I said in *Future Science,* Lawrence Beynam examined this vast subject and reported the following characteristics of the X-energy:

1. It is observed in the operation of heat, light, electricity, magnetism and chemical reactions, yet is different from all of them.
2. It fills all space, penetrating and permeating everything, yet denser materials conduct it better and faster, and metal refracts it while organic material absorbs it.
3. It is basically synergic. It has a basic negentropic, formative and organizing effect, even as heat increases, and there is the opposite of entropy (that is, disorganization and disintegration) as set forth by the Second Law of Thermodynamics, which it thereby violates.
4. Changes in the energy precede physical (observable) changes, and it is supposed to create matter, energy and life. This is also observed in certain psychic phenomena where metals continue bending long after the initiating agency/psychic has touched them.
5. It has its opposite number. Seen clairvoyantly by psychics as red and yellow, this energy is opposed to the life-giving energy outlined above. It can be seen when the life-giving energy is leaving, instead of entering (emerging into) a region. (For example, in Kirlian color photographs of a psychic healer's finger, the finger

is blue to begin with and then turns reddish-yellow when the healer transfers energy to a patient.) While the blue, synergic energy gives a cool, pleasant feeling to the sensitive, the yellow-red, entropic energy creates a feeling of heat and unpleasantness.

6. In any structure which is highly organized (e.g., crystals, plants, humans), there is a series of geometrical points at which the energy is highly concentrated (e.g., acupuncture points in acupuncture and chakras in the yogic tradition).

7. The energy will flow from one object to another. According to the Huna tradition, it is "sticky" so that an invisible stream of energy will always connect any two objects which have in any way been connected in the past (the basis of sympathetic magic). The energy is subject to exponential decay, radiating outward in the course of time from an inert material, but there is always a residue (since decay goes on to infinity). The density of this energy varies in inverse proportion to the distance; this ratio sets it apart from energies which obey electromagnetic and gravitational laws, but to this ratio a theory of potentials may be applicable.

8. The energy is observable in several ways: as isolated pulsating points, as spirals, as a cloud surrounding the body (aura), as a flame, as a tenuous web of lines (Don Juan's "lines of the world" and the occultist's "etheric web").

Huntsville, Alabama research engineer James Beal independently arrived at the same conclusion as Beynam's first characteristic of the X-energy. In a talk to the American Anthropological Association's 1974 symposium on parapsychology and anthropology, Beal noted that the effects should not be construed as the cause behind unexplained psychic events. According to him, some bioelectric field effects noted by conventional science may actually be "weak indicators, precursors, or stimulators in regard to effects filtering down from a higher system."

Dr. Harold Saxton Burr of Yale University was the discoverer of such an indicator system. His electrodynamic theory of life, first announced in the 1930s but still largely unknown to the scientific establishment, offers a solid link between electromagnetics and the mind—a bridge between the physical and the pre-physical foundations of life.

Burr's work, much of it done in collaboration with his student-colleague, Dr. Leonard Ravitz, shows that there is a guiding field which performs a directive, organizing function on the physical structure of an organism. This guiding influence is generally termed the L-field, short for life field. Burr and Ravitz demonstrated that the state of health of an organism could be determined far in advance of the least observable physical sign by using a microvoltmeter to inspect its L-field. Ravitz later learned that the L-field as a whole disappears *before* physical death. Sensitivity to the L-field might explain in part how psychic healers function in diagnosis and cure.

It is clear, however, that L-fields are themselves affected by higher-level forces. Ravitz made the further discovery that the state of *mind* (in the form of unspoken thoughts and images) affects the voltage gradients of the L-field. Edward W. Russell, in his book *Design for Destiny*, refers to this power of thought as a T-field, meaning thought field. He notes that although L-fields are ordinary electromagnetic phenomena, not a new force in nature, they are nevertheless of immense importance for showing how mind or T-fields can *measurably* affect L-fields and thus the physical body. L-fields give science a clear opening into that mysterious area where physics and psychology come together—the mind.

The concept of morphogenetic fields proposed by British scientist Rupert Sheldrake in his 1981 book, *A New Science of Life*, presents a widely-discussed hypothesis of "formative causation" postulating an invisible matrix or organizing field which regulates the structure, growth and behavior of all kinds of things. These fields are causative, serving as "blueprints" or guiding patterns for form and behavior of entities across time. This capacity is called morphic resonance. "When any one thing forms (a crystal, say) or any animal learns a new behavior, it will influence the subsequent learning of formation of all other crystals or animals of the same kind," Sheldrake says. He denies that the morphogenetic fields have energy; their influence seems to operate *ex nihilo*. Nevertheless, he proposes that psychic and paranormal events may be explicable by his hypothesis.

Although Sheldrake dispenses with all conventional forms of energy as the force behind forms, the data cited in this essay strongly suggests the reality of a new force in nature which could be the missing link which saves the morphogenetic field hypothesis from *ex nihilo* operation. In a personal communication to me, Sheldrake agreed: "When I say morphogenetic fields are nonenergetic, I do so to avoid confusion with the kinds of energy known to physicists. I hope that further research will indeed enable these problems to be resolved."

A concerted investigation of the fifth force or X-energy seems a promising research avenue to pursue in developing what Sheldrake terms "a new science of life and mind." He echoes Princeton physicist Eugene Wigner, who once wrote that "the present laws of physics are at least incomplete without a translation into terms of mental phenomena. More likely, they are inaccurate, the inaccuracy increasing with the role life plays in the phenomena considered."

This brings us back to the metaphysics which physicalism has so long denied and tabooed. It brings us beyond the physical into the realm of mind and suggests a promising avenue of investigation to pursue. In their search for an explanation, investigators of the psychic and paranormal should, of course, consider all which conventional science has to offer. But it seems that conventional science and parapsychology alike are "up against the wall" in their efforts to explain the paranormal—or, in the case of physicalists, to explain them away. Real progress is going to occur only when psychic and paranormal events are acknowledged and approached in a fresh and imaginative way. As Einstein once said, "The mere formulation of a problem is far more essential than its solution, which may be merely a matter of mathematical or experimental skill. To raise new question, new possibilities, to regard old problems from a new angle requires creative imagination and marks real advances in science."

In that spirit I have suggested the plausibility of a fifth force in nature and the need to investigate this hypothesized force. It is, from my perspective, one of the keys to explaining paranormal phenomena. In the next part of this essay, I will consider two others—the structure of space and the possibility of higher life forms.

From Parapsychology to Transpersonal Psychology

It is well known that the Swiss psychiatrist Carl Jung, one of the pioneers of transpersonal psychology, had a deep interest in psychic phenomena and paranormal events. He himself experienced them, and his concept of synchronicity was developed in an attempt to make rational what otherwise defied all scientific notions of reason and cosmic orderliness at that time. In his later years, Jung came to look upon physics as the field which could most profitably link with psychology to elaborate upon the concepts (such as synchronicity, archetypal experiences and the collective unconscious) which he himself had been unable to adequately articulate. In fact, it was Nobel laureate Wolfgang Pauli, one of the chief architects of quantum theory, who collaborated with Jung in his development of the synchronicity principle. (Arthur Koestler tells the story in *The Heel of Achilles*.)

Explorers of the unknown since Jung have recognized paranormal phenomena as points of convergence between psychology and physics—between our investigations of inner and outer reality. The paranormal turns out to be an opening into the larger question: What is reality and how can I know it?

Another topic which Jung pondered is UFOs or, as he called them, flying saucers. Although he felt their ultimate significance for people was psychological, he recognized their "psychoid"—a term he coined—nature, meaning they have quasi-physical characteristics as well and exist objectively in astrophysical space, where they could be photographed, seen on radar, and create physical trace marks on the earth. I feel that Jung was advancing in the right direction with such formulations, but that he didn't go far enough in explaining the interaction of mind and matter. In this section I will sketch the outline of what I think Jung, who died in 1961, would have concluded today in light of the data from parapsychology and ufology.

Exobiology suggests that life will begin almost anywhere in the universe, not just where conditions are favorable but where they are only slightly better than totally hostile. That being the case, and since the sun is a relatively young star, there is a high probability that life exists in stellar systems older than ours. In other words, there probably are more highly evolved life forms in the universe—higher consciousness, if you will.

At the same time that exobiology has been telling us this, the UFO scene has been intensifying. As I pointed out in *The Meeting of Science and Spirit*, UFOs and contactees are one of the focal points for investigators of paranormal phenomena. Some UFO contactees describe meetings with nonphysical entities who materialize into our three-dimensional space-time continuum from other sets of dimensions or higher planes of existence. Call them what you will—Space Brothers, metaterrestrials, ultradimensionals—their existence is said to be on a scale enormously beyond the human, just as ours is beyond that of insects, which in turn are similarly beyond microbes. From their level of reality, it is said, these higher forms of life influence and even guide human affairs.

It is interesting to consider that these notions of more highly-evolved entities match many of the descriptions of higher beings which we have from ancient religious and spiritual traditions. Are they merely the same ideas dressed in contemporary garb or are the reports of such beings valid and independent of those ancient traditions?

The Judeo-Christian cosmology tells us there are angels and archangels, cherubim and seraphim, inhabiting the heavens. And the term "heaven" is generally taken to denote a higher level of reality in the supersensible realm invisible to normal perception—a higher level of consciousness with its native life forms. In the Hindu and Buddhist traditions, the term for heaven is *loka*. Various entities inhabit the lokas also, notably the devas.

Deva is a Sanskrit term meaning "shining one" or "radiant being." It is conceptually equivalent to "angel." Devas have been described as belonging to another kingdom of life. They are neither animal, vegetable, mineral nor human. Rather, devas are a separately created order of life which has the role of supervising lower orders. Considered abstractly in scientifically-oriented terms, devas can be described as conscious, formative principles which guide and regulate life forms below them in the ladder of creation or the great chain of being, irrespective of space-time coordinates.

What has such supernaturalism and mythology as devic beings to do with parapsychology? I have already suggested the presence of a non-physical force in nature as the energetic mechanism producing psychic phenomena. Various ancient traditions identify it as the motive power behind paranormal phenomena. I've designated it the X-energy. Conventional science does not recognize the X-energy, but occult science does.

Grant for the sake of discussion that the X-energy exists. That is not sufficient to explain paranormal phenomena. Energy must be directed and controlled by a higher-level intelligence. Can the human mind exert such an influence? Parapsychology answers yes. For parapsychologists, some poltergeist phenomena seem plausibly explained as unconscious psychokinesis by living persons. Healing through the laying-on of hands is an example of psychokinesis through conscious, willed direction of X-energy. However, other paranormal phenomena appear to be of such magnitude that any intelligence presumed to be producing and controlling the energetic situation would have to be of a stature surpassing humanity by many orders of magnitude. The events at Fatima, Portugal, in 1917—popularly referred to as "the day the sun danced" but more soberly regarded as a spectacular UFO appearance—is such a situation. (See Jacques Vallee's *Dimensions: A Casebook of Alien Contact* for details.)

Are there such beings? As I point out in "UFOs and the Search for Higher Consciousness," a chapter in *The Meeting of Science and Spirit* and in *The UFO Experience,* exobiology suggests there are. Ufology and various spiritual and occult traditions also point with some degree of overlap at the notion of more highly evolved life forms whose existence is much older and grander than ours. Tie that in with noetics—which suggests that where life is, consciousness is—and the mystics begin to make sense when they say there is a hierarchy of conscious life forms leading up the great chain of being to the source of consciousness, God. (One astrophysicist speculated recently that pulsars—pulsating neutron stars—are intelligent beings. This brought to mind Edgar Cayce's statement that the sun may be an angel in another dimension.)

Now let's see how these two hypotheses—admittedly undemonstrated in scientific terms—might offer some explanation of paranormal phenomena and their relation to the human mind.

Recall our consideration of the terms "archetype" and "collective unconscious" in "Pole Shift Update" [in *The Meeting of Science and Spirit*]. Jung describes them this way in *The Archetypes and the Collective Unconscious:*

> A more or less superficial layer of the unconscious is undoubtedly personal. I call it the *personal unconscious.* But this personal unconscious rests upon a deeper layer, which does not derive from personal experience and is not a personal acquisition but is inborn. This layer I call the *collective unconscious.* I have chosen the term "collective" because this part of the unconscious is not individual but universal; in contrast to the personal psyche, it has contents and modes of behavior that are more or less the same everywhere and in all individuals. It is, in other words, identical in all men and thus constitutes a common psychic substrate of a supra personal nature which is present in every one of us.
>
> The contents of the collective unconscious are known as *archetypes.* [2]

Jungian psychologist Ira Progoff elaborated on his mentor's work in *Jung, Synchronicity and Human Destiny.* This passage is particularly relevant:

> The Self is the archetype of all the archetypes that the psyche contains, for it comprehends within itself the quintessential purpose behind the

impersonal archetypes and the archetypal process by which the ego and consciousness emerge. The Self may be understood as the essence and aim and the living process by which the psyche lives out its inner nature. As such the Self can never be contained by the ego or by any of the specific archetypes. Rather, it contains them in a way that is not limited by space or time. The way the Self contains the various contents of the psyche is in a kind of "atmosphere," a state that is more than psychological, an "aura" that sets up the feeling of this situation in a manner that is neither psychological nor spatial nor temporal. It involves something that can be spoken of as a nonphysical continuum by means of which the correspondences within the cosmos, the microcosm and the macrocosm, can come together to form patterns, at once transcendent and immanent, and constellating situations that draw physical as well as psychological phenomena into their field.[3]

Progoff's statement has many levels of affinity with various religious and spiritual traditions. The concept of a higher Self which is simultaneously immanent and transcendent is an ancient one. But this paradoxical statement about Jung's work also fails to cross the barrier of language which stopped Jung. It still doesn't integrate psychological concepts with physics as Jung hoped would be done. That is why Progoff had to put certain words in quotation marks. They indicate that the words are vague and imprecise. At best, the words are figurative and abstract, not literal and concrete. Where, for example, are archetypes stored in the brain? How are they transmitted from generation to generation? Saying they are encoded in the DNA molecule is unsatisfying because, even if finally proven to be so—and I doubt that it will—that materialistic position doesn't explain how *mental* experiences arise from *physical* combinations of atoms.

If we put aside the physicalist perspective and look in another direction, we see that parapsychology and ufology are beginning to offer some data with which to build a bridge between psychology and physics, between inner and outer space.

Kirlian photography, for example, shows that the corona discharge around a person—whatever the corona itself may finally prove to be—is subject to the thoughts of both the person himself and the thoughts of others, as in psychic healing. Photographing this energy through the Kirlian method shows dramatically that thoughts have immediate physical effects. In that regard, it is remarkably similar to the work of Burr and Ravitz.

In other words, there is an energetic dimension to thought or, as occultists and metaphysicians maintain, thoughts are things. The Burr-Ravitz data and Kirlian photography demonstrate the power of thought over physical matter and the visually observable level of reality.

Therefore I offer this speculation: If thought is energy (or at least has an energetic aspect) and if energy is neither created nor destroyed, then all the thoughts which have ever been thought are still in existence somewhere. Perhaps their form has changed; perhaps their energy content has dissipated. On the other hand, various esoteric traditions such as Tibetan Buddhism, Rosicrucianism, Huna and true magick say that, if the emotional component of a thought is sufficiently strong or if the intellectual component is sufficiently prolonged and concentrated, it may impress itself upon the nonphysical X-energy continuum in such a way as to create a thoughtform. A thoughtform (called a *tulpa* in Tibetan tradition) is an energetic embodiment of the idea on which the person focussed or dwelled mentally. Somehow it becomes disembodied and takes on an independent existence in physical space for a time. Its form and character accord with the thoughts and emotions of the mind (human or otherwise) which called it into being. (It is said, to elaborate this point, that when ascended masters appear physically in our level of reality, they "clothe" themselves in materialized thoughtforms drawn from the nonphysical X-energy continuum.) Dr. Gerald Langham of Fallbrook, California, a plant geneticist concerned with the relation between form and energy, coined the word "energysm" to denote phenomena of this sort. He says that an energysm is just as alive as an organism. If an organism is a being consisting of visible matter, he says, then an energysm is a being consisting of feelable energy which has not yet condensed to the state where it becomes visible to the naked eye.

An anecdote from Kumar Dilip Roy and Indira Devi's *Pilgrims of the Stars* illustrates this concept. The authors are yogis who recount their experiences on the yogic path. Indira possessed considerable psychic gifts, including clairvoyance. This gift enabled her to realize, she writes, "that many of the thoughts we take to be our own actually float in from the atmosphere and that it is our own free choice whether to accept or reject them."

Indira had a very vivid experience which taught her this. She was meditating in her guru's temple hall in Poona, India, with a group of friends. She could see very clearly that most of them had an aura of tension around them. They were concentrating so hard to silence their minds that it only heightened their awareness of thoughts. Not one person in the group was completely relaxed—the first necessary condition for meditation:

> Suddenly she *saw* a sex thought floating in from without and touching one person who accepted it. He became restless, but the thought developed in his mind in the form of jealousy, which is one of the concomitants of sex. He played with the thought and was soon carried away on the wave of a grievance and anger against the guru, the world and God.
>
> The thought touched two other people but as they did not give it a fireside seat, it quickly turned away from them. Another friend accepted the thought as his own and felt terribly anxious about his health.
>
> It was fascinating, though the whole thing did not take more than a minute.[4]

If this is so—that thoughts are real but nonphysical things—then perhaps human thoughts of a similar nature, or thoughts arising out of similar circumstances, may seek one another, coalesce and become what could be called a thoughtfield. Especially intense thoughts arising out of powerful experience from the collective history of the human race could then generate what Jung called an archetype, a psychic entity and (when consciously perceived) symbolic event in which certain deep experiences of our racial history are contained.

But notice, an archetype would then not be simply an idea in someone's mind. It would be a subtle repository of experience encoded in some energetic form *outside* the human brain/body. Its physical location would be the equivalent of an atmosphere around the Earth, not in the figurative sense which Progoff uses but in a literal sense. The archetypes would be an energetic shell or envelope, composed of some nonphysical energy—the X-energy—which surrounds the planet and which people have access to during dreams, meditation and other altered states of consciousness which lower our perceptual filters and allow our psychic senses to operate more fully.

Since archetypes are "universal" experiences, it wouldn't be rational to conceptualize them as spatially limited to a geographic area. Rather, they would be coextensive with the planet's physical atmosphere. How far outward they might extend is a problem which remains to be solved. And so is the problem of how information is encoded in such an energy envelope. But at least this conceptualization accounts for something which neurophysiologists and conventional psychologists can't explain, namely, how and where an archetype—or any other form of instinctive behavior—is "stored" in the brain. From the point of view of archetypes as energy thoughtfields, the "storage" is outside the brain/body. Both Dr. Elmer Green of the Menninger Institute and his biofeedback research subject, Swami Rama, support this position when they declare that their findings and experience suggest that "the brain is in the mind but not all the mind is in the brain." Green himself suggests the possibility of a "field of mind" around the planet. (The implications this concept raises about the nature of memory are, of course, on the same order as what I've just described about archetypal experience.) Furthermore, this concept relates directly to the conclusion reached in "Neuroscience and the New View of Mind."

What, then, is the collective unconscious? In terms of what I've developed here, it would be an energetic shell or envelope surrounding the planet, composed of all the archetypal thoughtfields created during human history—a field to which all people have access and which grows out of the historical experience of evolving humanity. (And it might well include the collective unconscious or racial memories of any other civilizations existing on Earth prior to our own—Atlantean, Lemurian, the "root races" of Theosophical tradition, and so forth.)

This conceptualization does two things. First, it satisfies Jung's requirements that the collective unconscious be both transcendent and immanent—beyond the individual yet within him—and the requirement that it must contain various contents of the psyche in a manner which is neither psychological nor spatial, nor temporal in the ordinary sense derived from physical science.

Second, this conceptualization supplements and supports the psi field theory of parapsychologist William Roll. It supports his theory by presenting a nonphysical but real means by which psychic sensitives may get extrasensory access to information about past human experiences.

Some psychics have given a description of how they operate in terms which parallel this conceptualization. Most notable was Mr. A, the anonymous but spectacular psychic healer (of Berkeley, California) whom journalist Ruth Montgomery wrote about in several books. Mr. A said he got his diagnostic information and healing energy from what he called "the ring"—something he described as a magnetic ring around the planet, and apparently not the Van Allen radiation belts.

I have extended the ring to become a sphere. And whether it finally proves to be a relatively localized sphere or some unlimited field extending throughout the universe, it at least presents a model of the occult concept termed "the Akashic record" which Edgar Cayce and other psychics have said they "read" in order to get psychic information. This model also agrees in part with the "cosmic computer" metaphor which some psychics and UFO contactees say is the source of their psychically-derived data. And it ties in nicely with Sheldrake's hypothesis of morphic resolution and morphogenetic fields.

Two Important Questions

But two important questions arise at this point. First, if this speculation is valid, how can we explain the way in which psychics obtain knowledge about the future, as well as the past? Second, does this conceptualization satisfy the requirements set down by spiritual traditions and transpersonal psychology for defining the nature of the higher Self?

It is clear that there must be more to the conception I've offered than just the foregoing if these questions are to be answered. At this point I suggest that the "something more" may include the notion of the noosphere proposed by the French Jesuit Anthropologist, Pierre Teilhard de Chardin (see his *The Future of Man*.) It may also include devas and angels.

Remember we have seen that there may be more highly-evolved life forms whose existence, occult and spiritual traditions maintain, is to some degree entwined with humanity as they influence and guide human affairs in the interest of evolving us to a higher state of being. From that point of view, the future of humanity already exists to some unspecified degree. That is because devic/angelic consciousness is characterized, among other things, by knowledge of the future since in some way it guides and organizes the human future. We ordinarily think of time as flowing from the past through the present to the future, but from the perspective I'm developing here, we could say that time flows from the future to the past—in the sense of the potential becoming actual. And devas, existing in a nonphysical but real form magnitudes of cosmological order beyond the human level, are of a still subtler or more rarified condition of being than the energy thoughtfields I've just called archetypes.

Devic/angelic consciousness thus interpenetrates the collective unconscious, and is co-spatial with it, just like water vapor and air. David

Spangler, one of the early residents of Findhorn, who claims to have channeled communications from devas and other forms of higher intelligence (see "Channeling and Higher Human Development" in *The Meeting of Science and Spirit*), told me that if the devas could be seen with unmediated vision, all that would be perceived is a shifting pattern of color and form.

What I am hypothesizing here, then, is an energy field surrounding our planet which has different densities or "planes" to it. Those densities or planes may be based on different gradations or forms of the X-energy spectrum. It seems likely that the energy or energies from which the devic/angelic kingdom emanates are of a higher order than the X-energy composing human thoughtforms.

Most probably, the energy field has both a static and dynamic aspect. In its static aspect, the collective unconscious grows infinitesimally over millennia as the pool of human mentality adds new psychic material—new information, images and concepts—to it. In its dynamic aspect, devic/angelic consciousness is in constant flux as it interacts with humanity.

Taken as a single organism, the energy field or field of mind might satisfy Teilhard de Chardin's description of the noosphere, which, he said, in one sense is still to be built but in another sense already exists. When he says "different senses," I feel I can specify them precisely. They have to do with different points of view—the human and the devic/angelic. From the latter point of view, the noosphere already exists because the devas and angels have it "in mind" for us and guide us toward its manifestation. From the human point of view, the noosphere is a-building as we ascend in consciousness and add our psychic contributions to the process which creates it.

The philosopher Oliver Reiser suggested there is a mutual induction process going on by which higher consciousness reaches down to humanity, while humanity in turn reaches up to higher consciousness. This conception of a two-way process for building Teilhard de Chardin's "spiritual earth" or what Reiser called "the psychosphere" would, I feel, adequately answer the two questions I raised about how psychics get future knowledge and also about the nature of our higher Self. Of course, the concept of the highest Self, God, is beyond all which I've sent forth here.

In this essay I have tried to show that physics and psychology (especially transpersonal psychology) come inexorably together in the study of paranormal phenomena. The meeting ground of inner and outer reality is consciousness, and paranormal phenomena turn out to be only a wedge into the more fundamental question: what is reality and how can I know it?

As I pointed out in "UFOs and the Search for Higher Consciousness," these questions about cosmology and ontology bring us to the realization that only by understanding the essence of ourselves—the "layers" of the psyche, including our higher Self and our highest Self—can we understand the nature and structure of the cosmos. And paradoxically, the deeper we look inside our personal self, the more transpersonal and universal we become. The split between mind and matter is healed through transcendence. Scientific and spiritual traditions—which are the objective and subjective aspects of our attempts to know reality more clearly—converge to reveal levels of consciousness far beyond what we ordinarily take for the limits of our awareness.

Where are these higher planes, these hyperspaces, these other dimensions? As I said in the UFO essay, all sources agree: they are within us, even though they seem to be outside us in physical space; and at the same time, they are indeed *out there*, even though we arrive there by going within through various psychotechnologies (such as meditation) for purifying personal consciousness and "cleansing the doors of perception." In this way we learn, as Jungian psychologist Marie-Louise von Franz has put it, that matter and psyche are merely the outer and inner forms of the same ultimate reality, consciousness: "...the ultimate components of matter present themselves to our consciousness," she states, "in similar form-structures like the ultimate or primordial ground of our innermost being."

The cosmos can be conceived as different but interpenetrating "levels" of consciousness, just as I've conceptualized our local planetary space as having interpenetrating layers of psyche. As a person expands his awareness, he passes through these different levels of consciousness en route to the highest state of consciousness. Those levels, I noted earlier, are called heavens, lokas, celestial spheres, zones of consciousness, etc. The terminology differs from culture to culture and tradition to tradition, but the underlying unity of experience can't be mistaken.

Each level is said to have beings native to it and capable of materializing into other, lower levels. As a person grows in mindfulness and develops "organs of higher perception," the boundary between "inner" and "outer" events dissolves. The subjective becomes objective. This is why there has been unanimity of reports from "soul travelers" to the highest regions.

And this is also why great spiritual teachers have calmly accepted the paranormal as quite normal and have displayed psychic talents far beyond anything seen in the laboratory. Think of Jesus healing the sick and raising the dead. Think of Sai Baba of India materializing fresh fruit out of season to feed the hungry. Think of Emmanuel Swedenborg telling someone about a fire raging in his home town as it was actually happening 300 miles away. Think of Rudolf Steiner clairvoyantly penetrating Hitler's mad scheme (as told by Trevor Ravenscroft in *The Spear of Destiny*) and mobilizing forces which were significant in the eventual defeat of the occult Third Reich.

From their higher level of consciousness, the supernatural is perfectly natural and mythology's symbolism turns out to be literally true. Both are concrete realities originating in a supersensible world, nonphysical but real, which has long been known to clairvoyants, seers and sages.

Does this mean that spiritual seekers should abandon science? Quite the reverse. The word *science* means "to know." The essence of science is its method, not the world view which has been built from a limited body of data obtained through the scientific method. The prevailing philosophy of science—mechanistic, reductionistic and atheistic—can be set aside without sacrificing what is valuable, namely, the scientific method. That method is an extremely powerful tool for investigating reality, and has already begun to give us technological means for objectifying what until now has been imperceptible to normal human senses. (See, for example, Appendix 5, "At the Borderland of Matter: The Case for Biological UFOs" in *The Meeting of Science and Spirit* and its expansion in *The UFO Experience*.)

But the scientific method is not our only way of knowing reality, and history has shown that science is no more powerful than the vision and imagination of those who use it. Has a century and a half of parapsychological investigations brought us any nearer to understanding paranormal events than those pioneering investigators who founded the psychical research societies? Yes, insights abound—but comprehension eludes us. Perhaps it is time, then, to take a fresh, innovative approach to the physics of paranormal phenomena. Perhaps it is time to take a more comprehensive view of existence—one in which we tentatively adopt the perspectives of our spiritual teachers, our primitive and occult traditions, our superpsychics.

This does not mean that scientists and researchers should forsake their rational faculties and intellectual integrity. Nor does it mean they should spend all night on a hilltop praying to a spacecraft (except, perhaps, as an attempt to follow Dr. Charles Tart's strategy for investigating states of consciousness.) That way madness lies.

But by adopting those world views as hypotheses for investigation, researchers into the paranormal will, I feel sure, navigate safely along that narrow, tricky path between having an open mind and having a "hole in the head." By remaining faithful to the scientific method without being bound by the worldview, prevailing among scientists, humanity will, I believe, see a flowering of the spirit of science leading to a science of the spirit.

And what would a science of the spirit be? Quite simply, it would be a commonly held higher level of knowing in which the nonphysical becomes objectified, empirical and publicly demonstrable. It would answer our questions about the physics of paranormal phenomena in a way which integrates our intellectual knowledge with our deepest feelings and most honored values in a life-supporting, life-enhancing manner. And in doing so, it would help to bring about a new social order which various spiritual and esoteric traditions envision—the New Age.

[1] Ivan Sanderson, "Editorial: A Fifth Force," *Pursuit,* Vol. 5, No. 4, October 1972.

[2] Page 3, Carl Jung, "The Archetypes and the Collective Unconscious," *The Collected Works of C. G. Jung.* Princeton University Press: Princeton, New Jersey, 1959.

[3] Pages 91-92, Ira Progoff, *Jung, Synchronicity, and Human Destiny.* Julian Press: New York, 1973.

[4] Page 252, Dilip Kumar Roy and Indira Devi, *Pilgrims of the Stars.* Delta Books: New York, 1973.

CHAPTER 3

THE MEANING OF SYNCHRONICITY

The word *synchronicity* was coined by the Swiss psychiatrist, Carl Jung, to describe a set of events which occur together in time and are meaningfully related, even though there is no recognizable causal connection between them. If you throw a rock into a pond, waves are formed; the rock causes the waves. However, if you are talking to a friend about a certain insect and that insect appears on your windowsill just as you are discussing it—as actually happened to Jung once—there is no apparent connection between the events in terms of conventional physics and biology, yet they appear to have a meaningful relation. They have an acausal connection.

The meaning of synchronistic events is not always clear, but they seem to arise from a higher-order reality. They seem due to a psychic force or an intelligence which transcends physical reality. They often give people an eerie sense that something vast connects their individual minds with the physical world to make things happen. They point beyond themselves to a greater significance. They raise the issue of free will vs. determinism, self-created destiny vs. fate.

Synchronistic events set us to questioning, to wondering, to searching for answers. The deepest dimension of synchronicity is its indication that a *telos*, a divine intelligence with a purpose, undergirds creation and that the universe is a teaching device to encourage humanity to search for ultimate meaning. That meaning is not synchronicity itself. Rather, it is beyond synchronicity—in fact, beyond all creation.

There is a 16th century woodcut which Jung liked so much that he included it in his book about the meaning of flying saucers. The illustration shows a robed man kneeling in wonder at the edge of a great inverted bowl on which stars and planets reside. That celestial bowl is the sky as we know it in ordinary, everyday life. However, the man's head actually projects through the hemisphere of sky and his face exhibits amazement because behind the hemisphere he sees a collection of gears and mechanisms which appear to be the "first cause" movers of surface reality.

A Breakthrough in Consciousness

I interpret the scene as illustrating the notion of a breakthrough in consciousness or entry into a mindstate which gives a clearer perception of reality. When all is said and done, synchronicity is only representative of an intermediate stage of higher human development. However, the enlightened person sees meaning in everything and knows that ultimately there are no coincidences because he has directly realized himself as one with the Cosmic Intelligence which governs creation through the hidden laws and principles of multidimensional, hierarchical reality.

The purpose of life—and that, after all, is what synchronicity urges us to seek—is to awaken us to ultimate reality, beyond all symbolism, beyond all partial representation, beyond all phenomena, beyond all space-time. There is purpose, meaning and direction to existence, and synchronicity is one of the means whereby we are impelled to discover it. Synchronicity is not an end in itself. It points beyond itself.

Human existence is characterized primarily by a progressive search for meaning. In the course of that search, people arrive at a stage of development known today as "soul-making." However, soul-making is less than ultimate. It is not the final stage of growth to enlightenment—it is the penultimate stage. It is transpersonal but not transcendent. Souls are not eternal, despite popular doctrines which say so. Even souls must ultimately dissolve into the void, and the enlightened being is one who has realized that, merging his or her individuality with

God so that no sense of egoic independence remains. Even "soul" offers a means for egoic attachment and individualized existence; hence it cannot be ultimate.

The ego undertakes the search for meaning because the ego is inherently unhappy and incapable of ease and rest. However, everything it grasps in search of fulfillment leaves it suffering—including synchronicity. The ego sees meaning in synchronicity but interprets the meaning as control. Ego sees synchronicity as a key to hidden knowledge offering a grander means of manipulating reality for its own gain, i.e., control. However, even that higher-level knowledge is insufficient to satisfy the ego. Only when the force of experience leads a person to recognize the inherent futility of trying to control the universe as if he or she were independent of it does the person find deeper meaning—the meaning toward which synchronicity truly points. That meaning is not control but self-surrender. Control is a personal experience; self-surrender is a transpersonal experience. Control of the universe is impossible; surrender to the universe is inevitable for all of us (one of these lives. ...).

In that surrender lies ultimate freedom. Synchronicity leads us from causality and determinism, through a recognition of the correspondences of "as above, so below," to liberation in which there is seen to be no ultimate difference between "above" and "below". As with the mystic poet, William Blake, we see heaven in a grain of sand and eternity in an hour. In that state of consciousness—enlightenment—we become co-creators with God and begin engineering reality rather than merely responding to it.

CHAPTER 4

CONSCIOUSNESS RESEARCH AND PLANETARY TRANSFORMATION

This chapter appeared as an article in *Atlantis Rising magazine* (May/June 2010).

Will the world end in 2012? Some authors—as well as some Hollywood producers—argue that, with predictions of catastrophic disasters ensuing from the convergence of planetary and cosmic cycles. Others expect the dawn of a New Age as the "gods" or ETs return to Earth.

All the hype and hysteria about 2012 is reminiscent of the hue and cry which emerged in the 1980s and '90s and the phenomenon called pole shift. My 1980 book *Pole Shift* covered the subject in depth, and the lessons I learned from doing that have relevance for the people who think 2012 will be "doomsday."

In the early 1970s, when I was working in California as Director of Education for the Institute of Noetic Sciences (founded by Apollo 14 astronaut Edgar Mitchell, the sixth man on the moon), there was a widespread rumor that the West Coast was going to experience a terrible earthquake and a large portion of it would "fall into the ocean."

This rumor was probably due to the psychic readings of Edgar Cayce, "the sleeping prophet." In the 1930s, Cayce had predicted vast changes in the geography of our planet. He called them "earth changes." There would be terrible earthquakes, volcanic eruptions, and the rise and fall of land masses, he said. They would begin in the second half of this century and increase in intensity, culminating at the end of the century in what Cayce described as "the shifting of the poles."

Over the years these predictions had permeated the psychic community and set up the expectation of terrible global destruction. Some people came to IONS with messages of that sort. The people were well-intended and simply wanted us to alert the world. I listened with interest to their warnings because part of the Institute's mission was to apply psychic functioning to planetary problems. But it wasn't our role to warn the public—civic officials do that—so I turned down all requests for help in publicizing forecasts of earthquakes, UFO landings and so forth. It proved to be the best policy because in all cases the predictions were wrong.

Nevertheless, my interest in precognition and psychic forecasting remained high, especially with regard to predictions of global destruction involving Cayce's notion of a pole shift. So in 1973, I began to investigate the subject. During six years of research, I gathered a large amount of data supporting the two principal questions I had asked myself: Have there been previous pole shifts? Might there be one in the near future? The evidence came from three sources: ancient prophecies, contemporary psychics and scientifically-oriented researchers. It pointed toward this conclusion: Yes, Earth had experienced pole shifts before and would again in the near future—at the end of the 20th century.

The pole shift concept indicates a sudden and radical displacement of the planet's axis of rotation or—an alternate view among pole shift theorists—a slippage of the planet's solid crust over the molten interior so that the polar locations change. Thus, "pole shift" means an event in which the North and South geographic poles move—as much as 180°, according to some sources—either because the planet tumbles in space, changing its angular position relative to the sun, or because the geographical points on the surface of the planet marking its spin axis are shifted due to crustal slippage. The time involved is said, by most sources, to vary from a few days to as little as a few hours.

What would result from a pole shift? It can be described as "the ultimate disaster." Enormous tidal waves would roll across the continents as the oceans became displaced from their basins. Electrical storms with hurricane winds of hundreds of miles per hour would sweep the planet. Tremendous earthquakes and lava flows would wrack the land. Poisonous gases and ash would fill the skies. Geography would be altered as seabeds rose and land masses submerged. Climates would change instantly. And if the shift were less than a full end-over-end, the polar ice caps, exposed to strong sunlight by having moved out of the frigid zones, would melt rapidly—within a few hundred years at most—while new ice caps would begin to build at the new polar locations. Last of all, huge numbers of organisms would be destroyed, including people, with signs of their existence hidden under thick layers of debris, sediment and ice or at the bottom of newly established seas.

In 1980 I published *Pole Shift*, which presented the evidence I'd gathered. (It is still in print.) But I said that presenting a case is not the same thing as proving a case. I pointed out that there was a strong case against pole shifts, there were many unanswered questions, and that I neither believed nor disbelieved the concept, but was simply raising questions as a journalist rather than giving answers as a scientist or psychic.

Beyond Pole Shifts

I continued to gather data bearing on the topic and by 1990 I felt a conclusion was clearly evident. I published a "Pole Shift Update" in *The Meeting of Science and Spirit*. I concluded that the pole shift concept is untenable; it is based on incomplete evidence and misinterpretation of data. I also concluded that the psychics who foresaw another one were wrong because the precursor events they predicted hadn't occurred, and the time for their occurrence was long past. The year 2000 came and went without the predicted disasters. Today, a decade later, it is more than obvious the predictions and prophecies were just plain wrong.

Does that mean there was no value to what I reported? Not at all. However, the significance is not in their literal or physical meaning, but in their symbolic or metaphysical meaning. Many of the predictions and prophecies go beyond a simple description of cataclysmic events. They also discuss the metaphysics behind those events, how they might happen, and why. In studying that aspect of the predictions and prophecies, we find a spiritual message of hope rather than despair, of insight into our own power rather than blind acceptance of a victim role.

Some people fearfully watched Earth's axis to detect the slightest indication of a pole shift. But that sort of behavior is self-defeating, the psychics and prophets say. We should be soul watchers rather than pole watchers because if there are people changes for the better, earth changes for the better will follow.

Let's consider the situation in more detail to see what the relationship between planetary well-being and human consciousness is said to be, as described by the esoteric psychology found in the pole shift predictions and prophecies.

All the world's major spiritual traditions tell us that free will operates in human affairs and that we can influence the outcome of events through the application of our physical, mental and spiritual resources. From the esoteric point of view, the purpose of prophecy is to warn people against the consequences of certain kinds of action. Dire prophetic words are spoken by a prophet to awaken people to their erring thought and behavior. By changing people's perspective and setting them into a new course of action, the prophet either diffuses the disaster-in-the-making or causes people to prepare for it sufficiently far in advance so that death and destruction are minimized. The people's new mode of behavior eventually proves the prophecy wrong or greatly moderates it—which is exactly what the prophet wanted in the first place!

The mechanism by which consciousness directly modifies a set of circumstances has been described by some of the psychics as "thought forms." The term and the concept behind it come from esoteric psychology and metaphysics. The concept posits a mental or psychic energy as an intermediate substance between matter and consciousness. From this perspective, thoughts are things—real but nonphysical energy configurations, produced by human consciousness—and they exist objectively in space outside the human beings who produce them. A thought form is the energetic embodiment of the idea on which a person dwells, consciously or otherwise, and it takes on an existence external to and independent of the thinker. By a process of which official science knows little, our thoughts, as a poet put it, "take wings."

In other words, when we think or focus our attention in a goal-directed way, the experience of thinking is not simply electrical activity within the neural pathways of the brain, nor is it confined to the limits of the cranium. Research into extrasensory perception and psychokinesis suggests a fifth force in nature which is beyond the four known physical forces and is senior to it. The fifth force is a metaphysical or mental force—a psychic force. Since energy can be neither created nor destroyed, presumably including this mysterious fifth force, a question arises: What becomes of a thought after it has been thought? Does it simply vanish?

From the point of view of psychics, metaphysicians, occultists, true magicians, shamans and so on, the answer is no. The energy of thought, they say, is still in existence as a sort of atmosphere or field surrounding the planet, recording all the experience of humanity. This is the so-called 'Akashic record' which Edgar Cayce and some other psychics claim to have 'read' when they obtained paranormal information about the past.

So thought activity, from the esoteric point of view, extends beyond the physical body. It partakes of a "field of mind" surrounding the planet and extending into space for an unspecified distance. The mind field is composed of the collective experience of the human race. That is, our thoughts, feelings and actions are somehow impressed or encoded into the field of mind energy, creating thought forms. Untold numbers of thought forms over thousands of years have been contributed by the human race to the planetary field of mind.

Moreover, thoughts of a similar nature tend to coalesce over time and gather into what could be called "thought fields." These thought fields are equivalent to what the Swiss psychologist Carl Jung called an archetype, which is a nonspatial, nontemporal repository of a certain basic human experiences. The totality of thought fields, or archetypes, constitute a kind of "atmosphere" of thought energy which extends through our planet's physical atmosphere and beyond. This nonphysical atmosphere can be understood as what Jung called the collective unconscious. The concept I am presenting here can explain in quasi-scientific terms how it is that people everywhere have access to archetypal experience, as Jungians and other schools of psychology claim. It is simply because we are all immersed in the collective unconscious mind field, which is suprapersonal.

Mind energy interacts with the physical energy matrix sustaining our planet in space, and can influence it, subtly but directly, in either a positive or a negative fashion, depending on the vibratory quality of thoughts arising from the human level. Harmonious, loving mental states are said to produce a stabilizing effect on the planetary matrix of physical energies; disharmonious, hateful thoughts result in a destabilized matrix.

This mind-matter interaction is a two-way process. People can "receive" from the planetary mind field as well as "give." For example, certain universal images and symbols have been perceived by people in dreams, meditation and other altered states of consciousness, regardless of the person's race, sex or culture. And for another example, consider how a new idea or discovery often appears almost simultaneously in several widely separated locations. Apparently, it happens to prepared or ready people as a result of "fallout" or "precipitation" from nonphysical levels of reality to the physical level.

Thus, the influence of our minds and our basic state of consciousness is there all the time, inevitably affecting the total Earth-organism, for better or for worse. It has been called *biorelativity*, the interaction of people with their physical environment via psychic or mind energy. The Hopi rain dance is an example of biorelativity—using the power of the mind to induce precipitation. The important question, then, is not *whether* we are going to affect the total Earth-organism, but *how* we are going to affect it.

In that regard, the predictions and prophecies say, virtuous living and respect for the planet will infuse Earth's energy matrix with powerful stabilizing influences. Prayer is a familiar form of this influence. It is no coincidence that psychic and spiritual traditions declare the effectiveness of selfless prayer. It adds constructively to the mindfield of Earth.

Even better still would be the development among people of a steadily focussed consciousness which recognizes the mutual dependence which humanity and the cosmos have upon each other as co-creators of our joint destiny. Such a loving state of consciousness would govern our thoughts and acts in a life-enhancing way.

Spiritual traditions warn that we shall reap what we sow. Esoteric traditions and psychical research offer an explanation of how and why this must be. Hatred, anger, greed, fear and other negative character traits and qualities of mind can affect the total process of energy activity on and around the planet. The many "crimes against nature" which people are perpetrating—such as environmental pollution, wasting of non-renewable resources, and nuclear testing—along with "crimes against humanity"—such as war, economic exploitation, and the imposition of inhumane living conditions, religious persecution, political abridgment of human rights, intolerance and bigotry toward minorities, and so forth—are all pouring negative thought forms into our planet's energetic foundations. The result, the predictions and prophecies said, would be geophysical cataclysm in the form of violent earth changes and a pole shift as the Earth-organism seeks to restore balance in the system.

So, from the point of view of psychic, prophetic, metaphysical and spiritual traditions, rather than saying we will be punished *for* our sins, it would be more accurate to say we will be punished *by* our sins. The law of karma, or cause-and-effect, is a stern one, so if there is some kind of "natural" global disaster in the future, to the extent that our own thought-energy is responsible for bringing it on, we will have no one to blame but ourselves.

Predictions of Global Disaster

Predictions of global disaster serve to point out that we must change our consciousness from ego-centered to God-centered living and recognize that there is a benevolent wisdom—a divine plan—lawfully governing the universe, including us. Moreover, many of the predictions declare that the severity—and even the possibility—of such disasters is influenceable by our manner of living and thinking.

From a spiritual perspective, there are no problems—there are only situations. Problems don't exist in nature. Only situations exist, only sets of circumstances. It is the human mind which projects attitudes and values onto those situations and then labels them as problems. But that label doesn't describe what nature is doing. It describes the state of mind of the human who labeled the situation.

Problems are a reflection of your state of mind—a state based on self-centeredness and fear and an unwillingness to face new experiences. But change your attitude and, suddenly, there are no problems. The set of circumstances remains, but the situation now becomes an exciting challenge in which to learn and deepen your understanding, your familiarity with the unknown. New values come into mind and are projected onto the situation so that what was once seen as a problem becomes a manageable situation and a fortunate opportunity for growth and discovery.

A global disaster such as a pole shift or some other massive earth change probably will not occur in the near future, but even if it does, we don't have to see it as a problem. We need not dwell upon it as a source of fear and destruction. Prudent, practical survival preparations can and should be made, of course. That's what civil defense, home preparedness and global warning networks are all about. That's what construction research and building codes are all about. That's why you don't build homes on fault lines or flood plains. Everyone reading this can think of recent events where, sadly, there was great destruction and loss of life, but which could have been greatly mitigated through civil engineering and social planning.

However, our primary task as citizens of Earth is to attune ourselves spiritually with Life—with the processes of the planet and the cosmos—and thereby understand that, if we seem to be *in extremis*, if we are entering a danger period, we are being given an occasion to grow, to evolve, to transform ourselves on the basis of deeper understanding and wider vision.

Spiritually speaking, we should remember the words of Jesus to be not anxious about the morrow, but rather to consider the lilies of the field which are arrayed in glory and are tended by a loving Providence who tends us every bit as well. To the awakened mind, every experience can be a blessing, even situations commonly labeled misfortune, tragedy, disaster, catastrophe, cataclysm. The attuned consciousness will receive all it needs, and more, from a loving universe whose whole purpose is to nurture the evolution of organisms such as us to a higher state of being.

I'll conclude with a brief story given to me by a wise man from India, M. P. Pandit, who read *Pole Shift*. He told me: One day Mr. Plague was talking to the Keeper of the Akashic Records when he remembered that he had an appointment at a distant city. So he broke off conversation and rushed to keep his appointment. When Mr. Plague returned from the distant city, the Keeper of the Akashic Records asked him, for accounting purposes, how many people had died on his mission. Mr. Plague replied, "Five thousand died due to me and ten thousand due to fear."

Think about that. According to the 2012 predictions and prophecies, humanity is approaching a critical juncture. Will there be global destruction or planetary transformation into a new world community of global cooperation and good will, a New Age based on love and wisdom?

The choice, according to esoteric psychology and metaphysics, is ours. The proper choice, the wise choice, is to shift our consciousness from the pole of egotism to the pole of enlightened living. We must realize that from the standpoint of God-realization, global cataclysms are merely an exotic way to die. The real question is: *Are we ready to die?*—period. Are we living our lives surrendered to God under all circumstances, even our own inevitable demise? Since the immortality pill hasn't been invented, none of us will get out of here alive. In pondering our mortality is the beginning of wisdom. If we do that, the pole shift predictions and prophecies—and other prognostications of global cataclysm such as those for 2012—will have served humanity and the planet alike by proving themselves "wrong" in the best manner possible.

Not so incidentally, when I was in the Yucatan several years ago, viewing some Mayan ruins, I asked my guide about the Mayan calendar ending in 2012. "What will happen then, according to your understanding?" I said. His reply was simple and straightforward: "I get asked that a lot. My answer is: Nothing will happen except the calendar will start over." No global disasters, no upheavals, no cataclysms. Life will go on.

I immediately related to that because it paralleled the pole shift predictions and prophecies. In my opinion, 2012 will come and go without the sort of cosmic calamities predicted. Sure, there could be some natural or social disasters, including geological, military and economic ones. They've been with us throughout history. But we're still here, evolving toward a higher state of being, as esoteric psychology and metaphysics encourages us. Consider, for example, the 14th century when the Black Plague killed an estimated one-third of Europe's population. Now contrast that with modern medicine and the current preparations to protect humanity against the H1N1 flu. Big difference! Big progress! Life will go on.

CHAPTER 5

CHANNELING AND HIGHER HUMAN DEVELOPMENT

This is a chapter from *The Meeting of Science and Spirit.* I have enlarged upon it slightly for this book.

Higher human development—evolution—has been accelerating in the last few centuries. The pace of change is now unprecedented for our species and what is to come is, I believe, a *new* species. We are witnessing the final phase of *Homo sapiens* and the simultaneous emergence—still quite tentative because of the nuclear and environmental threats to life—of what I have named *Homo noeticus,* a more advanced form of humanity.

It will take several centuries more to thoroughly demark the new age and the new humanity from the present one, and the transition will not be easy. Evolution never is. But as we pass from the Age of Ego to the Age of God, civilization will be transformed from top to bottom. A new, global society will be created—a civilization founded on love and perennial wisdom.

The change of consciousness underlying this passage involves transcendence of ego and the recognition of the unity of life in all its kingdoms—the mineral, plant, animal, human and spirit. However, information is necessary for transformation; there is no ascent into higher states of being without an attendant change in the content of consciousness. How does the human race get such information?

The expanding perimeter of human knowledge depends, first of all, on those courageous pioneers—those noetic heroes—who push into new territories of mind and new realms of reality. Through a combination of their own steadfast, selfless effort and divine grace from above, new understanding is gained, new information is revealed. Their experiences, their discoveries, their visions are then communicated to others through conventional means: speaking, writing and teaching. Slowly the word goes forth, drawing more and more people into sympathy and synchrony with the new understanding.

A second source of information for transformation is revelation. This is communication from nonphysical intelligences through people with special talent for receiving such transmissions. The modern term for such people is "channel," but traditionally they have been called oracles, mediums, trance communicators, shamans and other less precise terms such as visionary or seer (although the latter terms properly belong to those who achieved their insight primarily through spiritual practice rather than through the aid of nonphysical entities).

Channeled communications have a long and honorable history in human affairs. Of course, like anything else noble and elevated, they have their sleazy imitators and questionable claimants. Metaphysical bookstores are filled with books alleged to be from wise discarnates who, upon examination, don't speak two clear sentences in a row and who, if they were in physical form, probably couldn't walk and chew gum at the same time. These "revealed" works—however well intended—are generally a mixture of delusional fantasy and subconsciously recycled material from other sources which may or may not be genuine. In some instances there is deliberate intent to plagiarize, invent or commit fraud. For every Book of Revelation (John of Patmos said he received it from Jesus in his celestial form) there are dozens of revealed books not worth the paper they're printed on. The channels for such works are so bad in "audio" that we can be thankful they're not available in "video." Higher consciousness, it is not. As one perceptive commentator noted, both drinking water and sewage flow in channels.

Spiritual counterfeits aside, the human race has been uplifted by words of wisdom originating, it seems, from levels of existence beyond the human which are inhabited by more highly-evolved beings who are compassionately concerned for us and whose existence is, the communications say, inextricably entwined with our own. There is said to be a great variety of these superhuman and nonhuman forms of life: angels, archangels, devas, ascended masters and mahatmas, spirit guides, exusiai, cherubim, seraphim, extraterrestrials, metaterrestrials, ultraphysicals, Space Brothers and so forth. These entities and their native realms interpenetrate our own three-dimensional framework, creating a spiritual hierarchy, a great chain of being leading up to the source of creation, Godhead.

Whatever their name or form, the existence of these more highly evolved intelligences is on a scale enormously beyond the human, and from their level of reality they influence human affairs in a non-compulsory manner. From their point of view, the future of the human race already exists to some unspecified degree because they can see with overarching vision the possibilities ahead for us and can gently guide us toward desirable ends. Through a sort of mutual induction process, higher consciousness reaches down to humanity while, in turn, humanity—through its soul travelers, sages, saints and seers—reaches up to higher consciousness. Thus evolution proceeds.

Think of some examples of this:

- Moses heard a voice from a burning bush.
- Socrates had his daimon—a voice he perceived inwardly from childhood—which counseled him and offered prognostications.
- Saul, while journeying to Damascus to persecute Christians, heard the voice of Jesus and thereafter became St. Paul.
- Mohammed was given the Koran by dictation from the Archangel Gabriel.
- Nostradamus, in trance, received precognitive information from what he described as divine revelation, inspiration and good angels.
- Theosophy owes its existence to the discourses received by H. P. Blavatsky and several of her colleagues from discarnate mahatmas named Kuthumi and Djwal Kul, another ascended master, also known as The Tibetan, who produced numerous works through Alice A. Bailey.
- Edgar Cayce's readings were never clearly identified as to their source, but a number of indications suggest they originated at the transhuman level of existence called Overmind by Sri Aurobindo.

- Aurobindo himself began his spiritual development by trying his hand at automatic writing; his book, *Yogic Sadhana,* was written under the inspiration of Ram Mohan Roy, a deceased yogi who brought yoga to Great Britain in 1830. (Also, on two occasions in his early unfoldment, Aurobindo heard a voice from above commanding him to go to certain locations which were absolutely necessary for his safety, since he was being pursued by British authorities for his part in the Indian independence movement. He acted immediately, barely evading capture.)
- *The Urantia Book* is a collection of "papers" channeled during sleep by a Chicago physician in the 1930s; it is a gigantic work with many anticipatory insights into modern astrophysics and psychology.
- Krishnamurti, writing in his early teens under the pen name Alcyone transcribed *At the Feet of the Master,* claiming he merely recorded what was said to him by an ascended master while he, Krishnamurti, visited him during astral projection at night.
- Through the mediumship of Elizabeth ("Betty") White, a number of high-level discourses were received from discarnate intelligences whom she and her husband, Stewart Edward White, termed simply "The Invisibles"; her *Betty Book* and his *The Unobstructed Universe,* received from Betty through another medium after she died, are regarded as classics of mediumistic literature. The phenomenon continues today and increases at ever-faster pace. It is so widespread as to be a fad. Fads are usually superficial, however, there are many serious and notable examples of channeling which have helped give rise to the current public interest.
- While imprisoned in solitary confinement in 1973, Timothy Leary received a "Starseed communication" from what he termed Higher Intelligence; the communicator's point of origin seemed to be extraterrestrial. (Leary was a friend of mine and we corresponded while he was in prison.) The Starseed communication was reminiscent of the earlier communications which occultist Aleister Crowley claimed to have received from Aiwass, a native of the Sirius star system.
- Paul Solomon, a trance psychic in Virginia Beach, gives medical information about people in the manner which Edgar Cayce did; he speaks aloud, but without conscious recall—what is told to him by the Source.

- Aron Abrahamsen of Everett, Washington, also enters trance in a Cayce-like manner to produce health readings for people and even to locate objects and minerals in remote places.
- In the 1970s, Eileen Caddy and David Spangler of the Findhorn Community in Scotland channeled discourses from various non-physical entities—devas, angels and archangels—such as John and Limitless Light and Love.
- From the early 1970s a multidimensional being, Seth, spoke through the now-deceased channel, Jane Roberts, producing a stream of books, including the well-known *The Seth Material.*
- Likewise, *Jonathan Livingston Seagull* was written by Richard Bach after he heard a disembodied voice tell him the story; Bach says the voice, not he, is the real author.
- In 1981, a Westport, Connecticut, housewife named Meredith Young sensed a vibrational presence during meditation, followed by an urge to write. Three years later her channeled book, *Agartha,* presented the teachings of a group of non-physical beings who refer to themselves simply as Mentor, meaning teacher.

Perhaps the most spiritually pure and practical of all channeled communications in modern time are the text, student workbook and teacher's manual known collectively as *A Course in Miracles,* whose unnamed author is believed by many to be Jesus. (I do not subscribe to that view of its origin—as I explain in "The Meaning of the Christ" in *The Meeting of Science and Spirit*—but its beneficial influence on the lives of thousands of people is testimony to its divinely-inspired source.)

Determining the Source

But what *is* the source—not just of *A Course in Miracles* but of all channeled communications? Is it genuinely external to the psyche of the channel or is it an aspect of the channel's own mind?

The answer is ambiguous. It may be either; both are possible. You have to examine each case individually and even then "it" may not be perfectly clear. One of the greatest channels, parapsychologist Eileen Garrett, brought through several distinct channeled personalities, but after decades of experience and rigorous scientific investigation into paranormal phenomena, she was still not entirely certain of the source of her communications.

Discarnate benevolent entities of great wisdom are undoubtedly contacting humanity. Age-old tradition and contemporary experience attest to this. Likewise, the human potential for growth to godhood includes the capacity for people to utter inspired discourses from what esoteric psychology calls the High Self—the aspect of us beyond ego and individualism which is in touch with—even identical with—the transcendent dimension of reality. As I point out in "The Spirit of Creativity and the Creative Spirit" in *The Meeting of Science and Spirit*, many great artists have attested to the fact that their music, art, mathematical insights and so forth seem to come from a higher source. Even technological breakthroughs have originated in dreams and visions.

But the proliferation of channeled discourses today seems to far outnumber the discarnate entity population accessible by the people of Planet Earth. I guesstimate that perhaps 9 out of 10 channels are "bringing through" nothing more than a fabricated sub-personality of their own creation. Most of the material I see from channels is banal or trivial, stylistically awkward and often factually erroneous, such as the case I cite in *Pole Shift*, where an "ascended master" incorrectly stated that Arcturus is the pole star and that Earth has several magnetic axes. In a small portion of these instances there may be elevated speech, ennobling thoughts and sound psychological guidance, but it is nevertheless, as I evaluate it, simply a production of the individuals' self-unrecognized talent for subtle information gathering and theatrical dramatization, dressed up in the guise of some noble personality. This legitimizes the experience to the channel, who otherwise is not ready to accept it as an aspect of himself and to acknowledge the enormous creativity in the depths of his or her own psyche.

Now, there is nothing wrong with this capacity to channel in and of itself. In fact, development of it should be considered a positive step *if* the channel recognizes it as a manifestation of his or her own capacity to access the High Self. That Self transcends not only our own individuality but also that of discarnate entities, ascended masters, Space Brothers and so forth. It is the Ultimate Source of us all.

However, channeled information for personal growth—no matter how wise the information and regardless of the source—is useless for the channel until it is applied to his or her life. Trance channels rarely are aware of what they channel. For example, Edgar Cayce, until late in life, had no idea of what came through while he gave readings. (To his credit, Cayce did try to live in accordance with the principles enunciated in them.) I know channels who can give stunning information but who have to play back a tape recording of what they say in order to know what it is. Simply vacating your body while an entity speaks through you is *not* spiritual practice. The emptying of self which sacred traditions talk about results in mind*ful*ness, not mind*less*ness. For this reason, Theosophy frowns upon mediumship, even though it was part of founder H. P. Blavatsky's own experience. Likewise, Rudolf Steiner, the founder of Anthroposophy, declared that knowledge of the higher worlds should be obtained in the full light of waking consciousness.

A channel must recognize the indisputable fact that his or her own mind has a tremendous capacity for fantasizing, plausibly fabricating and spontaneously dramatizing something based on the slimmest data and subtlest cues. Why might a channel unconsciously fabricate? Escapism into fantasy, wish fulfillment, increased self-esteem, a subtle power trip— there are many reasons. The channel must beware and *be aware*. Reality testing is absolutely necessary, as I'll elaborate below. Without it lies the possibility of the channel succumbing to delusions of grandeur, depersonalization, multiple personality disorder and even spirit possession.

With it, ideally speaking, channeling can help a person to grow *beyond* channeling to the stature of a sage whose every word, however casually uttered, is full of wisdom and grace. There is no need for such a person to go through trance-induction procedures into an altered state of consciousness, assume a different personality and, after a period of effortful theatrics, resume an ordinary, colorless existence. Instead, the Source has infused the individual so fully that he or she can say, as Jesus did about his Father, that they are one. In *How to Be a Channel,* J. Donald Walters, formerly Swami Kriyananda, writes about his teacher, the renowned yogi, Paramhansa Yogananda: "...there was nothing ritualistic about his channeling, nothing portentous, nothing to make us feel that we had the rare blessing of being given ringside seats at some special and extraordinary event. He was so natural in everything he said, so unaffected, so seemingly casual, that, not infrequently, his most amazing statements almost passed unnoticed—only to be remembered later on with awe." I recommend Walters' sensible commentary and instructions on channeling.

Practical Advice for Channeling

It is not infrequent for people who are consciously on a spiritual path, following a tradition and practicing a discipline, to begin experiencing themselves as channels. It likewise can occur spontaneously for people not involved in such pursuits. What should you do if that happens?

The first thing is to remain calm. Don't panic; you're not losing your sanity.[1] Initial channeling experiences are analogous to visiting a foreign country with a very different climate, geography and culture. You need time to get used to it. While the experience can be disorienting at first, remember that you are simply gaining access to other levels of consciousness, other realms of reality, and learning to function in them.

Most spiritual traditions urge you to ignore or avoid developing such abilities, declaring them to be a trap or a dead end. The path to God doesn't depend upon such experiences, the traditions maintain. Enlightenment is direct God-realization—beyond all mediated knowledge from discarnate sources who, however advanced they may be, are not ultimate. Krishnamurti came to understand this; later in life he abandoned the practice which led to *At the Feet of the Master,* saying there was no need to seek enlightenment through an occult hierarchy. "Truth is a pathless land," he declared. A wise friend, experienced in occultism and channeling, put the same thing to me differently when, pointing heavenward, he said, "Straight up with no tangents."

If you decide to use channeling as a spiritual tool—and it can be a useful one—you must exercise discernment, discrimination and caution, at least as much as you would for more earthly forms of human activity. There are distinct dangers.

One of the great soul-travelers with profound knowledge of inner space, the eighteenth century Swedish mystic-philosopher, Emmanuel Swedenborg, said, "When spirits [meaning low, not angelic, ones] begin to speak with a man, he must beware that he believes nothing that they say. For nearly everything they say is fabricated by them, and they lie—for if they are permitted to narrate anything, as what heaven is and how things in the heavens are to be understood, they would tell so many lies that a man would be astonished. This they would do with solemn affirmation. ... Wherefore men must beware and not believe them."

Spiritual traditions warn us to "try the spirits" and test our visions to see whether they are truly from God. Jesus put it simply: By their fruits ye shall know them. It is easy to be deceived by ego-created fantasies, hallucinations and delusions. Likewise, the unwary can fall prey to deceptive messages and messengers. Low-level entities lurk in metaphysical realms, ready to rush in where fools tread. Sensible use of channeling requires a high degree of character development and a balanced, well-integrated personality. Without that, the channel can run into difficulties such as spirit obsession and even possession.

Several recent books offer valuable guidance in the matter. I've already mentioned Walters'. Jon Klimo's *Channeling: Investigations on Receiving Information from Paranormal Sources* is the most scholarly and comprehensive, covering the history and theories of channeling; it also offers instructions on how to channel and how to do so safely. William Kautz and Melanie Branon's *Channeling: The Intuitive Connection* is less theoretical and more how-to, but no less sound in its advice and spiritual perspective. Last of all, I recommend Corinne McLaughlin's *How to Evaluate Psychic Guidance and Channeling.* This brief pamphlet is available from the School of Spiritual Science, Sirius Community, Baker Road, Shutesbury, MA 01072.

To put my cautionary advice in a few sentences, here are what I see as the primary questions to consider in testing the nature, orientation and spiritual quality of channeled communications:

ARE THE COMMUNICATIONS COMPATIBLE WITH THE BODY OF SCIENTIFIC KNOWLEDGE? If not, why not? Even genuinely new knowledge will at least be compatible, however revolutionary or advanced it may otherwise be. For example, some UFO contactees claim to have been given predictions of world-shaking events and are urged by the aliens or extraterrestrials to make them widely known. Many contactees have done so. Almost invariably the predicted events don't occur, leaving the contactees looking foolish for having made their public statements. This is a pretty good indication that the entities are either figments of imagination or astral tricksters—or worse.

Beyond that, you must understand that any finite being is not omniscient, no matter how far up the spiritual hierarchy it may be. Even the most highly evolved spiritual figures—incarnate or otherwise—can overreach themselves and make mistakes. Sometimes it may be a statement which is demonstrably false or is at least open to debate and differing interpretation by others who, although not equally evolved in consciousness, are nevertheless qualified with regard to the particular topic or issue.

ARE THE COMMUNICATIONS COMPATIBLE WITH THE TEACHINGS OF THE WORLD'S MAJOR RELIGIONS AND SPIRITUAL TRADITIONS? Again, if not, why not? Is recognized spiritual authority and the collective experience of thousands of years to be lightly ignored? Remember that such wisdom and authority comes from people who, like you, were searching for spiritual truth.

All sacred traditions have made explicit warnings about psychic phenomena (including channeling) and have formulated doctrinal statements and instructional statements to guide practitioners safely along the path to enlightenment or God-realization. Remember: psychic development is not the same as spiritual growth.

DOES THE COMMUNICATOR RECOGNIZE A HIGHER POWER? Anything which claims in personal terms to be ultimate, isn't. If you are a Christian, ask whether the communicator recognizes the spiritual authority of Jesus. If you belong to another tradition, ask about the highest authority of that tradition.

IS THERE PATIENT REGARD BY THE COMMUNICATOR FOR YOUR OWN SENSE OF TRUTH AND YOUR NEED TO TEST THE VERACITY OF THE COMMUNICATIONS? Meredith Young was told by Mentor, "You must trust us based on your reaction to our teachings." This concern for the channel's sense of truth is an important indication of the benign nature and trustworthiness of the communicator. The other sort may begin speaking sweetly, but soon the tone changes and becomes demanding, frantic and hostile.

DOES THE COMMUNICATOR ASK PERMISSION TO CONTINUE COMMUNICATION? Seeking permission is a sign of respect. If the communicator does not ask permission, if it shows no regard for the integrity of the communication channel, beware. I know people who have experienced communicators breaking in on them without warning, day or night, whether the person is prepared or not, alone or in a group. This sort of entity will disrupt activities, creating havoc in daily affairs and frightening anyone around, alienating them from the channel, who appears to be—and, in fact, is—out of control.

DO THE COMMUNICATIONS ENCOURAGE YOUR OWN GROWTH TO INDEPENDENCE OF THE COMMUNICATOR AND OTHER EXTERNAL AUTHORITIES? Kyros, an entity channeled by Sandra Radhoff of Lakewood, Colorado, recently stated, "A good channel is one who attempts to guide others into the awareness of their own abilities to connect with their own higher guidance. But many [people] move from channel to channel (from Ramtha to Lazaris to Mafu) like that which are termed 'groupies' following rock stars... Some entities depend on channels to tell them what to do in their lives or to tell them what will happen in the future." It should be clear that such dependence is only a step away from addiction, and spiritual addiction to anything other than God is as detrimental to higher human development as physical addictions are. A meditation junkie, a bliss ninny, a spook chaser is still an addict. That is not the same as God-intoxication.

If your channeling doesn't pass all these tests, I suggest you close down that line of communication altogether. (There may be other entities whom you've learned to trust and whom you can safely continue to bring through.) Your mental health could be at stake.

Channeling, when done properly, can be a valid means of spiritual growth, and the spiritually-aspiring person should welcome whatever assistance he gets along the way, whether from ordinary or extraordinary means. For some seekers, it is not the channeled communications which are important but rather the experience of opening themselves in love and trust to a higher reality; for others, however, the important thing is the harsh experience of having the glamour removed from their illusions about spirituality and higher consciousness when they find their much-valued channeling capability has led them into foolishness or worse.

Whatever the case, it is important to recognize that psychic communications are merely signposts pointing the way for the spiritual traveler; they are not the ultimate destination. The destination is the Kingdom of God, the Transcendental Domain.

You see, the very act of communication presumes some kind of separation—a split or division between sender and receiver—and it presumes some kind of knowledge to be transmitted from one to another. Communication of any sort is at best a bridge, and a bridge presupposes some degree of separation between the parts being connected.

The Kingdom, however, is union with God—the transcendence of all sense of separation or gulf between God, humanity and the cosmos. Spiritual traditions tell us that our true identity is the One, the Whole, which manifests with infinite variety but which is never anything less than the all-in-One-and-One-in-all. It is profoundly mysterious, and although people can name it and talk about it, the reality of it is beyond all knowledge which can be verbalized. It can never be adequately communicated; it can only be experienced. It can never be comprehended; it can only be apprehended.

Therefore, the best channels contacting the highest source are not those which produce words, but deeds. Channeled information is useful and valuable only if it leads to human transformation; otherwise it remains merely a philosophy or a curiosity. As Karl Marx said (and we can appreciate it without being Marxist): philosophers have sought to explain the world; the thing to do, however, is change it. Authentic channeling—whether from discarnate entities or from a person's own High Self—involves a dimension of reality which seeks to go beyond communication—to communion. It seeks to transform people and, indeed, human society itself. Is that not, in its ultimate sense, precisely what the coming of the Kingdom is all about?

We are all, therefore, called by Universal Mind to be channelers in the service of higher human development. We are called to transform ourselves and to assist others in that process. Words can be important in that regard, but deeds are more so. Channeled words aplenty abound; there is a surfeit. But the channeling we are truly called to do—the channeling most needed today by a groaning planet—was described elegantly in a simple prayer. It is wisdom I wish to conclude this essay with—the Prayer of St. Francis:

> Lord, make me a channel of your peace.
> Where there is hatred, let me sow love,
> Where there is injury, pardon,
> Where there is doubt, faith,
> Where there is despair, hope,
> Where there is darkness, light
> And where there is sadness, joy.
>
> Lord, grant that I may seek to comfort rather than be comforted,
> To understand than be understood,
> To love than be loved.
>
> For it is in giving that we receive,
> It is in pardoning that we are pardoned,
> And in dying that we are born to eternal life.

---

[1] Actually, you're *gaining* your sanity by losing your everyday view of reality which, insofar as it has excluded spirit realms, is itself insane—in the sense that anything less than a clear view of ultimate reality is to some degree crazy. Ideal mental health is the condition known as enlightenment. Short of that, we're all insane to one degree or another.

CHAPTER 6

MY NEAR-DEATH EXPERIENCE

This was published in *Vital Signs*, Vol. 14, No. 2, Spring 1995. It is the newsletter of the International Association for Near-Death Studies. I have added a new conclusion for this book.

The near-death experience is a crash course in spirituality and the human potential to expand consciousness. My interest in spiritual experience and the nature of consciousness has been present from early childhood, but a near-death experience at age 14 certainly accelerated it. As one of the founders of the International Association for Near-Death Studies in the 1970s, I obviously have a deep and abiding interest in the subject. I've written and lectured about NDEs from a theoretical, research-oriented perspective and about the experiences of others for more than two decades. However, I've never written about my own near-death experience until now. I chose to keep my personal life out of my writing in order to direct readers' attention to my work rather than to me. However, I'm often asked about my personal experiences. Therefore, after twenty-plus years of writing about altered states of consciousness and noetic studies, I've decided to be more public about myself, so I've written this brief account.

In 1953, during my fourteenth summer, I nearly died through drowning. The event was completely unnoticed by anyone. I'd gone swimming at a pond about a mile from my home in Cheshire, Connecticut. At the time, Mixville Pond was my town's only public swimming area, although there was no lifeguard on duty in those days. I rode my bike there one sunny afternoon and swam out to a platform which had a diving board. The platform was about six feet above the surface of the pond and the board added perhaps a foot more height.

I'd come by myself and didn't meet any friends there. The beach wasn't very crowded. The platform was empty, but a few people were sunning themselves on a nearby raft. Feeling the vitality of youth, I began to dive in a show-off manner. It's not that I was a great diver; I was simply enjoying the feeling of performing more than routine, simple dives as my body responded to my intention of "swan dive," "half-gainer," "back flip."

After a few of those, I decided to do what I'd heard called a "sailor dive." As an adult, I now know there is no such thing, but somehow I'd gotten the false, foolish notion from some friends that sailors dove headfirst with their arms next to their sides rather than in front of them. So I did that. I sprang on the end of the board and sailed high in the air to enter the water head-first at a very steep angle of descent and with greater-than-normal speed gained through attaining more-than-usual height.

Near-Death through Near-Drowning

It was a really stupid thing to do. I plunged through the water toward the bottom and went deeper than usual—so deep, in fact, that I struck my forehead on the sandy floor of the pond. The shock of the blow passed through my body at lightning speed and I lost normal awareness. I was blacked out on the bottom, unconscious. If I'd been monitored by an EEG and an ECG, some vital signs would have showed, of course. My heart continued to beat and my brain kicked in the drowning reflex which closes the windpipe (trachea) so water can't be inhaled to the lungs. It's the opposite of the gag reflex which forces a person to cough up something in his trachea which is preventing normal breathing. The wisdom of my body said: Don't breathe!

I know that now, looking back. However, at the time, my understanding was quite different.

I lay unconscious on the bottom of the pond for several minutes. I'm estimating that duration on the basis of two things. The first is book-knowledge of how long it takes before irreversible brain damage sets in from lack of oxygen. It's generally said to be four to five minutes. In cases of drowning, that may be extended, depending on the temperature of the water. The colder, the better; bodily processes slow down greatly in icy water, but this was mid-summer.

The second is from contests I held at that time with a friend during English class, when we'd sneakily challenge each other to hold our breath while the second hand of the clock crept around once, twice and, for me—because I usually won—a few seconds more. At that point I'd have to give up and breathe, so I know I could hold my breath for at least two minutes.

As I rested on the bottom, my awareness changed from blank nothingness to a sensation of wonderful, warm tranquility and security. I had no external perception, no sensory awareness. I was simply floating idly, feeling more peaceful than I'd ever been. And while that languor and serenity pervaded me, I had the fascinating experience of "seeing my life pass before my eyes," as the saying goes. That life review wasn't sequential; it was more like all-at-once, yet each scene was nevertheless discreet. I didn't watch it, strictly speaking—I lived it, I was in it, experiencing it rather than passively viewing it. Yet I also knew that it had all happened earlier and that I was really reviewing it. There was a strange, simultaneous subjectivity and objectivity to it.

My visual field—if I can call it that—as I watched my life pass in review was unlike normal vision, which is limited to about 120 degrees in front of you, including peripheral vision. But my life review was a full 360 degrees! I could see everything around me, front and back. And even as I objectively "saw" all that, subjectively I felt all that as if it were happening to me for the first time.

Not all the features of the idealized NDE which researcher-authors Raymond Moody and Kenneth Ring have identified were present. I didn't float out of my body and go down a dark tunnel toward the light, nor did I sense the presence of a being of light or an otherworldly environment. Moreover, I didn't feel judged, nor did I feel a profound reorientation of consciousness from sin and guilt, although it was clear from the review that I'd sometimes acted with shameful self-centeredness. But remember, I was only 14; I didn't have all that much life to review.

Return to Life

As I drifted at ease, feeling a vague sense of satisfaction, I slowly became aware of a pounding in my ears. Then I became aware of my chest heaving, trying to breathe, but no air moved into my lungs. I developed a strong sense of danger and started to panic. No light penetrated to the bottom of the murky pond. Everything was dark so I was quite disoriented.

Then my hand brushed the bottom and immediately I had a sense of direction. I kicked my arms and legs wildly to swim to the surface, yet they hardly seemed to move, so close was I to paralysis. Amid that action I thought rather calmly *I'm drowning.* There was an impossible pressure in my lungs. They swelled up, trying to take in air, but the airway-stoppage reflex was still active. I moved through the water for an agonizing time until at last my head broke the surface. I was surprised to find that I could see but I still couldn't breathe, so powerful was that life-saving reflex. I couldn't cry for help. In fact, I was so traumatized that I could hardly control my arms and legs enough to tread water. The people dozing on the raft didn't notice my plight.

Somehow, through the grace of God and a strong will to survive, I remained above water while my airway opened enough for me to begin breathing again. I slowly, wearily swam to the raft, hauled myself up the ladder with great difficulty and lay down to rest, exhausted. After about ten minutes I felt well enough to swim to shore. Then I got on my bike and rode home.

I never told anyone about the event until many years later when my writing brought me in touch with Ring, Moody and several others who were focusing their research on the near-death experience. Why didn't I mention it, at least to my parents? Strangely, it didn't immediately seem important. I had survived; I was 14 and full of boyhood concerns. So I sort of tucked it away in memory, where it worked like slow-acting yeast in a bowl of bread dough.

The Gift of Nearly Dying

Now, as I look back on that experience of nearly dying, I am infinitely grateful for it. It introduced me to the power of consciousness and the hidden dimensions of human life. Since then I have experienced deeper, fuller, spontaneous alterations of consciousness which have impelled me to practice more deliberate means for expanding awareness, realizing ultimate values and maturing in character. However, the seed-energy of that NDE was planted and grew. I can summarize it with this quote from my book, *The Meeting of Science and Spirit* (pp. 218-219):

There is no way to enter the Kingdom except to ascend in consciousness to the Father, to that unconditional love for all creation which Jesus demonstrated. That is what the Christian tradition (and, indeed, every true religion) is all about: a system of teachings, both theory and practice, about growth to higher consciousness. But each of us is required to take personal responsibility for following Jesus on that way. That is the key to the Kingdom. Self-transcendence requires honesty, commitment and spiritual practice to cultivate awareness. The result of such discipline is personal, validating experience of the fact that alteration of consciousness can lead to a radical transformation of consciousness, traditionally called enlightenment. But this, by and large, has been lost to the understanding of contemporary Christendom. Instead, Jesus and the Bible are idolized, and heaven is said to be located somewhere in outer space. Awareness of inner space—of consciousness and the need to cultivate it—is sadly lacking. Exoteric Judeo-Christianity must reawaken to the truth preserved in its esoteric tradition.

For example, the original form of baptism, whole-body immersion, was limited to adults. It apparently was an initiatory practice in which the person, a convert who would have been an adult prepared through study of spiritual disciplines, was held under water to the point of nearly drowning. This near-death experience was likely to induce an out-of-body projection such as many near-death experiencers report today. The baptized person would thereby directly experience the transcendence of death, the reality of metaphysical worlds and the supremacy of Spirit. He would receive a dramatic and unmistakable demonstration of the reality of the spiritual body or celestial body of which St. Paul speaks in I Corinthians 15:40-44 (apparently referring to his own personal experience with out-of-body projection). The conventional forms of baptism practiced today—even those involving bodily immersion—are, from the esoteric perspective, debasements of the original purpose and meaning of baptism in the Judeo-Christian tradition. (However, I am not implicitly advocating a return to that esoteric practice; much safer, less risky methods of inducing out-of-body projection are available today. The present symbolic use of baptism is justifiable if it is supplemented with the necessary understanding of its true but esoteric significance.)

Added Conclusion

Because of the transformative effects of the near-death experience, some recent research has focused on the social structure of the non-terrestrial environment in which NDEs occur and its sociocultural relevance for humanity. One investigator asked: "Do these visions and values of the Good Life bespeak a renewed desire for some lost Arcadia or golden age? Or do these visions in the final moments of consciousness reveal, at death's door, a final yearning for utopia?" Both questions presume a psychological origin in the human mind. However, I do not think the answer is simply either/or. I think it is a both/and. The "and" is this, stated as still another question: "Or are they clear perception of another realm transcendent to physical reality?"

NDEs and the Ideal Society

NDE visions reveal, at death's door, the ideal society. They are, in my judgment, clear perceptions into a transcendent, metaphysical realm which is senior to our familiar 3-D space-time reality and which, in the great chain of being, influences and guides our development in the physical realm. Call it the shaman's imaginal world, Plato's Theory of Ideas, the yogic model of reality, Judeo-Christianity's heavens, Hinduism-Buddhism's lokas, Taoism's World of the Immortals, Islam's Garden of Paradise, Native America's Happy Hunting Ground—whatever the name, the universality of the notion of reality as multileveled, with various planes of being affecting those "below" them, is what makes sense of NDE visions of a transcendent society.

Yes, there are cultural overlays which the NDErs unconsciously place on their perceptions while out of their bodies in the NDE-world. However, an underlying commonality more fundamental than cultural overlays can nevertheless be discerned by noetic researchers.

All the world's great religions, sacred traditions, hermetic philosophies and mystery schools agree that the senior realms—collectively, the metaphysical world—have beings who are native to those realms and whose nature is to interact with humanity in some way. Some beings apparently are malevolent, but the benevolent ones whom NDErs perceive as beings of light are my concern here. Although their social organization is not entirely apparent in all details, it is nevertheless clear that they themselves are models for human aspirations of spiritual growth. Call them angels and archangels (Judaism, Christianity and Islam), call them devas (Hinduism and Buddhism), call them ascended masters in their solar bodies (mystery schools), call them cloudwalkers or Immortals (Taoism), call them those who have attained the resurrection body and the company of saints (Christianity)—these beings present themselves to us in ways which appeal to our deepest nature and which urge us to externalize that nature in every aspect of our being, including relationships and social organization. They are a transcendent society, an order which exists beyond, but alongside, our own.

Bridging the Worlds of Matter and Spirit

However, it appears that the "membrane" dividing Nature and its inhabitants into a physical realm and a metaphysical realm is permeable in a two-way fashion. NDErs penetrate it spontaneously through nearly dying, but psychics, mystics, shamans and seers such as Emanuel Swedenborg, Rudolf Steiner and Edgar Cayce penetrate it in a controlled, deliberate fashion.

Likewise, those who die biologically often report seeing into a nonterrestrial environment in their final moments, as Drs. Karlis Osis and Erlendur Haraldsson showed in their important study, *At the Hour of Death.* The 1979 book presents findings from interviews with more than 1,000 doctors and nurses in America and India—two widely diverse cultures—who report strikingly similar perceptions by the dying. Those deathbed visions include apparitions of human and nonhuman figures such as Jesus and Krishna and scenes or landscapes of nonearthly nature. As Osis said to me, "The experiences of the dying are basically the same, regardless of culture, education, sex or belief system, and their experiences cluster around something which makes sense in terms of survival after death, and a social structure to that afterlife."

"As above, so below" is a metaphysical axiom. Christianity preaches the kingdom of heaven, Tibetan Buddhism has its Shambhala and other traditions have their images of human perfection and the ideal society, but these images are not simply "all in the mind" as conventional psychology would have it, i.e., fantasy, wish fulfilment, projection. Rather, as esoteric traditions and transpersonal psychology would have it, there is only one great 'Mind,' and what we experience as most deeply personal is actually universal. In that sense, these images are indeed all in the mind, but only because the deepest layers of the human mind are coterminous with the ultimate structure of the cosmos. What some call the highest state of consciousness is another way of describing the ontological ground-structure of reality. Therefore, the pursuit of the ideal society is a perennial project for humanity and will be until our evolution has brought us back to godhead—the same godhead which began the cosmic drama of our evolutionary unfoldment and which, paradoxically, we are right now and have been all along, but without recognizing it.

NDE = Nearly Done with Evolution

Insofar as NDEs awaken us to our true identity, the acronym could be said to stand for "Nearly Done with Evolution." However, evolution is not the same thing as instant transformation. Living in accord with the spiritual guidance obtained during an NDE is hard work requiring profound personal change. It takes time, patience, commitment and courage to integrate the experience. NDErs often express anger and frustration with their return to life because their exalted experience is not understood by those around them and, even worse, is sometimes scornfully rejected.

Moreover, the experience itself is not ultimate. As I noted, nearly dying can be a crash course in spirituality (to those whose NDE involved a vehicle wreck: no pun intended), but it's only one course, not complete graduate school. NDEs are enlightening but not final enlightenment. In terms of Patanjali's yogic model of consciousness, an NDE is equivalent to savikalpa samadhi or samadhi-with-form, i.e., a visionary experience involving the subtle plane of existence in which the experiencer still has a separate sense of self. Beyond that, however, is nirvikalpa samadhi or formless samadhi, a causal plane experience of self-as-cosmos in which there is no separation. However, even that is not ultimate. Beyond it is sahaj samadhi, "easy" samadhi or "open eyes enlightenment" in which all that arises within one's awareness is seen as simply a modification of God, the One-in-all-and-all-in-One. Beyond sahaj samadhi are even higher states (see my forthcoming *Enlightenment 101: A Guide to God-Realization and Higher Human Culture*).

In terms of the mystery school tradition, an NDE is equivalent to the first initiation (which in ancient times could have been baptism or whole-body immersion). It leads to the state of consciousness characterizing Homo noeticus. The disorienting after effects which NDErs experience are due in part to their lack of preparation for initiation.

There are higher initiations, however, and they go beyond the form of the NDE into the formless. Adeptship, the culmination of mystery schooling, is far beyond the first initiation.

Beyond Homo Noeticus

Adepts are what I have in mind as models of higher human development—the Jesuses, the Buddhas and other enlightened men and women of history who delineate the characteristics of what I see as the coming race, Homo noeticus, and beyond that to Homo magnus. Beyond even that, it seems to me, are the beings of light met during NDEs; they are enlightened to a still-higher degree, that of actually *being* light, and likewise exemplify a still-further stage of our future evolution which I call Homo illuminatus. The beings of light whom we meet in near-death conditions are, from my perspective, representatives of a state which awaits humanity in the future—a stage of evolution I term "merged" and characterized by the light body as the vehicle through which they function.

Homo noeticus is such not simply because s/he has awakened the heart—a quality wonderfully exemplified by NDErs. S/he also has awakened the wisdom-eye. The love of Christ, the compassion of Buddha is balanced by wisdom. Without wisdom, transpersonal love or what Christianity calls agapé can become "sloppy agapé"—mere emotionalism or indiscriminate, foolish behavior which turns people off to what NDErs want to share with them. NDErs have a distinct calling to live in accordance with the ideals they experience during near-death, and that is fine. However, they are returned to life and Earth to make the ideal real. To real-ize who we are means living from the wisdom-eye as well as the heart.

So it is no wonder that NDErs are less than fully realized divinity. The ultimate yardstick was stated simply two millennia ago: "By their fruits ye shall know them." By that I do not imply any criticism of NDErs; I merely mean that we all have a long way to go, and the spiritual journey proceeds at a slower pace than many would like to think after coming back from an NDE. However, the amount of frustration, impatience and anger we feel with others for not understanding our NDE-based reorientation to life is a direct measurement of the amount of ego left in us.

CHAPTER 7

WHEN PANDORA'S BOX
WAS OPENED...

This chapter is the Afterword to my book *Psychic Warfare: Fact or Fiction?* (Aquarian Press, England, 1988.) Its sub-title is "An investigation into the use of the mind as a military weapon."

According to Greek mythology, Pandora was created by the gods, who bestowed their choicest gifts upon her and fashioned her to counteract the blessing of fire stolen by Prometheus from heaven. When Pandora opened her jar—the legendary "Pandora's box"—all manner of evils flew out over the earth. Hope alone remained inside, the lid having been shut before she could escape.

Psychotronic weaponry (PT) appears to be one of the worst evils ever released upon humanity. If the reality of it is only a small part of the terrible potential envisioned by some of the preceding authors, it will still be bad enough to rank as a major threat of human welfare.

Yet, as a poet (Alexander Pope) wrote, "Hope springs eternal in the human breast." PT technology is, after all, only technology. As such, it has potential for good. Its beneficial application is prevented only by the minds, the ethics (or lack of them), the consciousness of those who control it. As I noted about true magick in the Introduction, the

69

mind-machine interface called psychotronics can be used to bless or to curse, to help or to hurt.

And there is reason to hope. For psychotronics can be seen as a case of the glass being half-full rather than half-empty. Time after time history has shown an awakening of human conscience to the misapplication of technology and its inherent threat to planetary well-being. Dire predictions and Cassandra-like prophecies serve their purpose, which is to awaken people to impending disaster so that action is taken to divert the course of society in time to avoid it, or at least moderate its severity.

The same may occur in contemporary world affairs. Although the level of danger and destruction is likely to increase, there are clear signs of countervailing influences at work on a host of global problems, from food production and population growth to depletion of natural resources, pollution of the environment and proliferation of nuclear arms. The voices of reason, intuition and prophecy are being heard.

Perhaps psychotronic technology will ultimately be used for peaceful, creative purposes rather than the warring, destructive ones. That is the hope of some who are deeply involved in psychotronic research. They see beyond the ego and its self-aggrandizing extensions into culture. They recognize genuine human needs and are pondering the benevolent possibilities inherent in the new technology to relieve human suffering, enlarge human comfort, provide basic necessities in a democratic fashion and elevate—even inspire—human awareness to new heights of visionary caring.

In that vein, let's consider briefly some hopeful possibilities for psychotronics.

Medicine may be the first area in which psychotronic technology is applied on a large scale. Reports from experimenters and holistic health practitioners state that radionic devices can cure disease or alleviate organic disorders, regardless of distance between the patient and the device. The Priorè machine, invented in France, is the center of controversy there because advocates claim to have cured incurable cancers, and the national government has some degree of evidence supporting the device's efficacy.

Apply the same technology to agriculture and the result is pest control and enhanced soil condition. Exactly that has been claimed by some agricultural experimenters, who report improved yields of higher quality because of radionic crop treatment. The importance of such a possibility for alleviating world hunger is obvious.

And since hunger is worst in Third World, underdeveloped nations, the first need there is a plentiful supply of inexpensive electricity. Psychotronics offers a benign source of power production. The controversial electric motor of Joseph Newman, highly publicized in the press when he challenged the U. S. Patent Office, is an example of what is to come. There are probably more inventors in this field working on "free energy" devices than any other application—and being strongly opposed by the status quo, whose commercial interests would be at stake. Imagine, for example, an inexpensive home unit that allows people to energize circuitry with electricity derived from "zero-point" energy. The electric utility industry's investment in huge fossil, hydro-power and nuclear generating plants, transmission and distribution lines, and supporting facilities would all become unnecessary.

Free energy devices might also reduce international tensions. As "have" and "have not" nations find wealth more equitably distributed and as the comfort level of underprivileged societies improves, the explosive conditions which breed political discontent and instability would be defused. The threat of military actions to secure, for example, Mideast petroleum for the West would be eased.

At the same time, eliminating nuclear power plants would eliminate the problems of radioactive waste disposal which might pollute underground water sources. A more immediate threat from nuclear power is the possibility of meltdowns or accidents of lesser degree resulting from operator error or failure of safety systems. This, too, would be eliminated by free energy devices.

Air and space travel would likewise be revolutionized by psychotronics. The UFO phenomenon, insofar as it represents an advanced propulsion technology, is probably psychotronic in nature. The qualities of UFO propulsion include the ability to cross millions of miles of space, travel through Earth's atmosphere at speeds in excess of 16,000 miles per hour (some have been clocked on radar), perform right-angle and complete-reverse turns as if pivoting on a point, ascend directly for thousands of feet with near-instant acceleration to maximum atmospheric speed, and so forth—all apparently without a conventional fuel source. Electrogravitation seems to be the medium used by UFOs, which have been observed to dematerialize and rematerialize. This being so, imagine what the effect of such technology would be upon commercial airlines and airports.

Think also what the effect of the foregoing would be on the global problem of atmospheric pollution. If coal and oil-fired electric generating stations become obsolete, if the petroleum industry is replaced as the fuel supplier for air and ground transportation, one consequence would be massive reduction of polluting emissions. A clean-up of atmospheric pollution—no more acid rain, no holes in the ozone layer—would occur naturally through the elimination of major pollution sources.

In addition to purifying the atmosphere, psychotronic technology offers means for weather control and engineering. Since the pioneering days of Dr. Wilhelm Reich's "cloudbusting" efforts in the 1950s, his technology has been extended and refined, primarily by Trevor James Constable, to the point where regional meteorological conditions can be engineered. Rain and other forms of precipitation, clouds, wind and lightning have been created and abated through unusual PT devices. In one instance a large-scale heat wave was broken through PT weather engineering. The ramifications of such operations for agriculture, aviation, recreation and public safety are enormous.

Remote viewing for location of minerals, oil and other natural resources is still another possibility envisioned by psychotronics inventors and technicians. A forked stick, angle rod or pendulum in the hands of an expert dowser is a simple but effective form of psychotronics usually applied only on site, although some dowsers claim to locate water or missing objects through dowsing a map first. More sophisticated devices which amplify the power or sensitivity of the operator could be used with correspondingly amplified results.

These are only some of the applications of psychotronic technology that hold the promise of promoting a peaceful world providing abundantly for its human inhabitants, who in turn would be treating it with respect and understanding of its deeper dimensions—dimensions where humanity transcends its traditional divisions and false identities in the growing awareness of unity-in-diversity and the sacredness of life. In the words of the 1981 Survey of Science and Technology Issues Present and Future, noted in the Introduction;

Attempts in history to obtain insights into the ability of the human mind to function in as-yet misunderstood ways goes back thousands of years. Only recently, serious and scientifically based attempts have been made to understand and measure the functional nature of mind-mind and mind-matter interconnectiveness. Experiments on mind-mind interconnectiveness have yielded some encouraging results. Experiments in mind-matter interconnectiveness (psychokinesis) have yielded less compelling and more enigmatic results. The implications of these experiments is that the human mind may be able to obtain information independent of geography and time ... A general recognition of interconnectedness of minds could have far-reaching social and political implications for this Nation and the world.

PART 2

UNDERSTANDING THE SPIRITUAL

CHAPTER 8

JUDEO-CHRISTIANITY AND THE PARANORMAL

This originally appeared in *The Meeting of Science and Spirit* (Paragon House, 1990).

The Holy Bible is a veritable storehouse of psychic lore and tales of supernatural events. The paranormal is integral to the Judeo-Christian tradition, but its ultimate significance is not that it provides evidence of unseen realms in the cosmos or of untapped powers in the human race. Those are real, but phenomena in and of themselves are not ultimate, whether the phenomena are called psychic, paranormal, supernatural, transphysical or miraculous. Spiritually naive people may become fascinated with such phenomena—it may be awe due to simple ignorance or it may be power-lust due to egotism—but for the mature person whose life reflects the presence of what is traditionally referred to as the Holy Spirit, paranormal phenomena always point beyond themselves to their source, God.

The god of the Bible is, of course, the Living God and thus the Holy Spirit, as an aspect of God, is a living being. That does not mean, however, that the Holy Spirit is a person or a ghost (even a holy one) or—as some religious art depicts—a dove. Those familiar conceptions are intended symbolically, but when taken literally they become misconceptions or misunderstanding of God—spiritual truth seen "through a glass darkly." The Holy Spirit does not have any form which human thought can conceive.

For the modern mind, nurtured in a scientific culture, the Holy Spirit can best be understood as the universal power through which God performs miraculous or supernatural events. It is one of the modes the Divine uses to operate in the universe. As such, it is the matrix or field from which all psychic or paranormal phenomena are generated. Properly understood, then, paranormal phenomena are instances of a general condition: the Power of the Living God, the Force Field of the Life Source. Those phrases are closer to the terminology of science, but they are only contemporary expressions for the more traditional term, Holy Spirit.

Ideally, then, the psychic and the paranormal realms draw us toward a deeper understanding of the nature of reality. When Jesus performed miracles, he always pointed beyond himself to the source of his power, God. So did the Hebrew prophets.

Jesus and the Hebrew prophets taught people that God is the source of creation and that our personal power, our life—indeed, our very being, including our post-mortem existence—is a miracle freely granted through God's unconditional love. Their teachings sought to counter the materialistic views and values which ignored or denied the presence of Holy Spirit, and their paranormal demonstrations served to reinforce that realization in people. The teachings and demonstrations asked: What have we done—what *can* we do—to deserve the gift of life, the abundance and happiness which is ours when we yield ourselves wholly to God? The answer is: absolutely nothing. Life itself, they implicitly said, is the ultimate paranormal event and the Love, the Creative Power, the Life Force which brings it forth is wondrous. Recognize that and give thanks to God for the amazing grace which sustains us and the entire universe moment to moment, eternally. It is a miracle beyond comprehension.

That is the significance of the paranormal in the Judeo-Christian tradition. It has perhaps been said most elegantly and succinctly in the poetic prose of *A Course in Miracles:* "Miracles occur naturally as expressions of love. The real miracle is the love that inspires them. In this sense everything that comes from love is a miracle."

CHAPTER 9

MEDITATION AND EVOLUTION

This chapter is an expansion of the Introduction to my book *What Is Meditation?* (Anchor-Doubleday, 1974).

Life on Planet Earth is threatened from many directions; many responsible sources warn of this. There is the possibility of nuclear, chemical and biological warfare by the superpowers. There is worldwide pollution of the air, land and sea by all nations. Nonrenewable resources—topsoil, water, various minerals, tropical rain forest and the ozone layer, for example—are being wasted or destroyed. Over-population is straining the biosphere, bringing drought and pestilence.

All these threats to life are man-made; all of them originate in the minds of people. Our behavior is a manifestation of our thinking and emotions, and in turn our thoughts and feelings are dependent upon our state of consciousness. Our present world situation, then, is one in which we exhibit much irrational behavior. That, in turn, is due to what we might call "a crisis of consciousness." If so, the solution to the problem presented by these threats can be stated very simply: *change consciousness.*

Survival demands a change of consciousness. Not just survival, either, but also evolution. As I read the history of nature, I see evolution as a record of evermore complex forms of life coming into being in order to express more fully the consciousness behind life, indeed, behind all creation. The history of evolution is a story of creating evermore complex forms of life displaying evermore complex consciousness, from unicellular organisms through plants and animals to the human species.

Evolution is always at work. That means now, today. And what I see today, in addition to the threats to life, are signs that the life force itself is mobilizing its resources to resist extinction. How will it resist? The answer is simple: by evolving forms of life which are suited to the new conditions on Earth—forms of life which know how to live in harmony with the planet and its creatures. They will know how to live this way because their consciousness will have changed.

"They" in-the-making is us. If we have seen the "enemy"—human irrationality—we also have seen the possibility of participating in the evolutionary process and changing ourselves in a conscious, self-directed fashion. Meditation is one of the means to help ourselves make the necessary change of consciousness which a New Age demands. Meditation is a means of personal and transpersonal growth. Meditators claim that the best way for people to change is by "working on yourself" from within via meditation. It is a time-honored technique— perhaps humanity's oldest spiritual discipline—for helping people to release their potential for expanded consciousness and fuller living.

As a technique for assisting in the enlightenment process of knowing God or ultimate reality, meditation appears in some form in every major religious tradition. The entranced yogi in a lotus posture, the Zen Buddhist sitting in zazen, the Christian contemplative kneeling in adoration of Jesus, the Sufi dervish whirling in an ecstasy-inducing trance: all can be properly described as practicing meditation. Although the cultural or religious trappings may vary, meditation's core experience is an altered state of consciousness in which the ordinary sense of "I"—the ego—is diminished, while a larger sense of self-existence-merged-with-the-cosmos comes into awareness.

Meditation Research

Meditation works on all levels of our being: physical, psychological and social, as well as spiritual. Research shows that it improves general health and stamina; it decreases tension, anxiety and aggressiveness; it increases self-control and self-knowledge. Drug use and abuse are usually curbed, and sometimes even stopped. Psychotherapy progresses faster than usual. Personal and family relations seem to improve. And except for borderline psychotics, meditation is safe, harmless, extremely easy to learn, beautifully portable, available in endless supply and completely legal.

Meditation research has been reviewed by Michael Murphy and Steven Donovan in their very valuable book, *The Physical and Psychological Effects of Meditation*.[1] It covers scientific research, from the first meditation study in 1931 through 1988, and summarizes what has been found to happen, physiologically and psychologically, during and after meditation sessions. Murphy and Donovan show that most claims for meditation are valid, so far as the first stages of meditative activity go. Although more and finer research is needed, they say, to look at the "greater heights and depths of transformative experience," research to date corresponds with traditional accounts by meditators sufficiently well enough to suggest that "the ancient paths toward enlightenment produced the kinds of integration and illumination they claimed."

Gains from Meditation

There will never be a better world until there are better people in it. Meditators claim that meditation changes their lives for the better. Edgar Cayce described meditation as an emptying "of all that hinders the creative forces from rising along the natural channels of the physical man to be disseminated through those centers and sources that create the activities of the physical, the mental, the spiritual man; properly done [this] must make one stronger mentally, physically..." (Reading 281-13) Dr. Haridas Chaudhuri, philosopher-author of many works on spiritual development, defined meditation as "the art of bringing to full flowering the hidden spiritual potential of man's psychophysical system."

Although enlightenment is the ultimate goal, many meditators (perhaps most of them) will not reach this fulfillment—at least in this lifetime. Nevertheless, if you begin meditating, you can be reasonably certain that you will still find many worthwhile benefits in your life. These are likely to include (1) freedom from the feeling of pressure in

---

[1]   *The Physical and Psychological Effects of Meditation*, Michael Murphy and Steven Donovan. Esalen Institute, 1988. Available from The Esalen Study of Exceptional Functioning, 230 Forbes Avenue, San Rafael, CA 94901.

day-to-day affairs, (2) avoidance of what is generally called "that tired feeling," (3) minimal recurrence of chronic nagging pains such as headache, arthritis, indigestion, and colitis, (4) reduction of insomnia, caffeine and nicotine dependence, and general use of drugs, (5) greater tolerance and love for others, (6) greater satisfaction from your religious affiliation, if you have one, and (7) greater desire to be helpful, either in public service or in your own private life.

In the more advanced states of meditation, mental and physical stillness is complete. The meditator is totally absorbed in a blissful state of awareness having no particular object. His consciousness is without any thoughts or other contents; he is simply conscious of consciousness. In yoga, this emptiness of consciousness without loss of consciousness is called samadhi. In Zen, it is satori. In the West it is best known as cosmic consciousness or enlightenment. And there is a paradox in this; in the emptiness comes a fullness—unity with divinity, knowledge of humanity's true nature and, to use a phrase from St. Paul, "the peace of God that passeth all understanding."

Lama Anagarika Govinda, a German who became a Tibetan Buddhist lama, said that meditation is:

> The means to reconnect the individual with the whole, i.e., to make the individual conscious of his universal origin. This is the only positive way to overcome the ego-complex, the illusion of separateness, which no amount of preaching and moral exhortation will achieve. To give up the smaller for the bigger is not felt as a sacrifice but as a joyous release from oppression and narrowness. The 'selflessness' resulting from this experience is not due to moral considerations or pressures, but a natural attitude, free from the feeling of moral superiority; and the compassion which flows from it is the natural expression of solidarity with all forms of sentient life.

Definitions and Techniques

That experience of peace and unity is difficult to attain, however, because the mind is always wandering. Meditation might be described as a technique for developing attention control so that worry, fear, anger and all other anxieties gradually dissipate. The dictionary definition of meditation, based on Western psychology, is inadequate to describe this experience. "To contemplate" or "to ponder" is not synonymous with meditation as a spiritual practice. Going further in the diction-ary, we find a better sense in which it may be understood, namely: "a form of private devotion consisting of deep, continued reflection on some religious theme." This is closer to the true meaning, but still is not completely adequate to explain meditation.

In physiological terms, meditation is neither ordinary waking, sleep-ing nor dreaming, but rather what has been described as a "wakeful hypometabolic condition." Brainwaves, heartbeat rate, blood pressure, respiration, galvanic skin resistance and many other body functions are altered in meditation. They slow to the point achieved in deep sleep, and sometimes beyond, yet the meditator remains awake and emerges from meditation with a feeling of rest and loss of stress and tension. All this certainly is not included in the dictionary definition of meditation.

The common core of all meditation experiences is an altered state of consciousness which leads to a diminishing (and, hopefully, a total elimination) of ego, the self-centered sense of "I". This core-experience has been called "relaxed attention," ""nonanxious attention," "detached alertness" and "passive volition."

To attain this state, many forms and techniques of meditation have been developed. Some are passive,—for example, when a yogi sits cross-legged in a lotus asana with so little motion that even his breathing is hard to detect. Other forms of meditation, such as tai chi, involve graceful body movements. Sometimes the eyes are open; sometimes they are closed. Sometimes other sense organs than the eyes are emphasized, as when beginners in Zen pay attention to their nasal breathing. In other traditions, however, sensory withdrawal is dominant; attention is taken away from the senses. Some meditative techniques are silent; some are vocal. Transcendental Meditation is an example of the silent form while the Krishna Consciousness Socie-ty uses the "Hare Krishna" chant (which means "Hail, Lord Krishna"). Some meditations are private and some, such as a Quaker meeting, are public. And although most forms of meditation are self-directed, sometimes they are guided by a group leader.

Silent Forms of Meditation

The silent forms of meditation center on three techniques: concen-tration, contemplation and the mental repetition of a sound. The sound, called a mantra, may be a single syllable such as Om. It may be a word, phrase or verse from a holy scripture. The Tibetan Buddhist *Om mani padme hum* (meaning "the jewel in the lotus" or enlightenment) is an example. So is the simple prayer in the book called *The Way of A Pilgrim* which goes, "Lord Jesus Christ, have mercy on me." Many Christians use the Lord's Prayer as a basis for meditation. Saying the prayers of the rosary is likewise mantric meditation. The Indian sage, Kirpal Singh, taught his followers to silently repeat five names of God which he gave them in a ceremony. Likewise, Maharishi Mahesh Yogi and his teachers of Transcendental Meditation initiate people into TM with various Sanskrit mantras; the meditator then uses his mantra during his meditations. Zen Buddhism has a variety of meditative techniques, some of which involve use of a koan, that is, an apparently insolvable riddle which the meditator silently examines. A widely-known koan asks, "What is the sound of one hand clapping?" Another inquires more directly about the basic nature of self-identity: "Who am I?"

In contemplative forms of meditation, the eyes are open so that the meditator sees what is called in Sanskrit a *yantra*, a form on which he centers his attention. The focus of attention may be a religious object such as a crucifix, statue or picture. It might be an inscription, a candle flame, a flower. They all serve the same purpose. Or the meditator may use a *mandala*, a painting or drawing, typically a square-in-a-circle design of many colors, which symbolizes the unity of microcosm and macrocosm.

Concentration is generally considered the most difficult form of meditation. In concentration techniques, an image is visualized steadily in the mind. It could be the thousand-petaled lotus of the Hindu and Buddhist traditions or the crescent moon of Islam. It could also be Judaism's Star of David or Christianity's mystic rose. Alternatively, the mind may be held free of all imagery and "mental chatter"—a clearing away of all thought. Or the attention might be focused upon some part of the body. For example, the mystical "third eye" at a point midway between the eyebrows is often used. (This is said to coincide with the pineal gland.) Also common is the so-called "concentration on your navel." This phrase is actually a misunderstanding of the process of directing attention to the abdominal area about two inches below the navel and simply becoming one with your breathing. The meditator flows into awareness of the rhythmical, cyclical body process by which life is sustained and united with the universe.

Some disciplines combine different aspects of several meditative techniques. For example, some styles of the martial arts use meditation in their training regimen. The Russian mystic Georges I. Gurdjieff taught his students to combine movements and meditation. Psycho-therapist-author Dr. Ira Progoff of New York City guides people through therapeutic sessions using a techniques he developed called process meditation. It is usually performed in a group, and he speaks in order to guide the meditators into exploration of whatever imagery appears in their minds.

So meditation cannot be defined in a sentence or two. The term means many things to many people, varying in this or that aspect, depending upon culture, religious traditions, psychological orientation, the individual's purpose and other factors.

Experience Is What Matters

In meditation, it is not really the definition but the experience which matters. Historically, the goal of meditation has been a transformation of the whole person. Research data, as I said, dramatically validates many of the claims which meditators make. Traditionally, these behavioral changes are reinforced through voluntary conformity with the meditative ethos and lifestyle—an aspect still little researched by science. Throughout history, teachers of meditation and spiritual masters have emphasized "right living" to support one's meditation. By that they mean a healthy diet; an honest means of income; association with virtuous and sympathetic people; truthful speech; kindness and humility in relations with others; a social conscience; giving up egotistical desire for power, fame, prestige, wealth, psychic powers, and so forth. As psychiatrist, Arthur Deikman, points out:

> Probably the importance of meditation lies in its changing a person's orientation toward living, not in its ability to produce dramatic changes in states of consciousness. It's fairly easy for a normal person to have 'unnormal' experiences, but people meditating without the supporting philosophy are less likely to be involved long enough for some of the subtle changes to occur or to change their orientation from doing to allowing things to happen spontaneously.

This does not mean, however, that successful meditation requires extreme asceticism and withdrawal from society. The true aim of meditation is to bring the meditator more fully into the world, not to retreat from it. A religious retreat may be appropriate for some in the course of their meditative training and discipline. This is an honorable tradition—the way of the anchorite, monk, nun and religious devotee. Yet even renunciate monks and nuns living reclusive lifestyles often undertake efforts of a social nature—feeding and clothing the poor, for example, or offering spiritual sustenance to the ignorant and uneducated.

Here it is also important to note that meditation does not require abandonment of the intellect. It is true that in meditation the intellect's limitations become apparent, and other (usually unsuspected) modes of creative problem-solving and insight emerge. However, enlightened teachers, even illiterates such as the Indian yogi Ramakrishna, have always been recognized as brilliant people with finely-honed intellectual powers who have enhanced their meditation "research" through study which cultivates the mind. Their writings and discourses display clear logic, a keen analytic discrimination, and a knowledge of tradition. It is no accident, then, that students frequently report improvement in their grades and ability to study after beginning meditation.

The best which can happen through meditation is enlightenment. Spiritual masters of all ages have been unanimous in declaring that through meditation, people can come to know God. Through direct experience—not through intellectual conceptualization—people can reach a state of conscious union with ultimate reality and the divine dimension of the universe. In that state, all the long-sought answers to life's basic questions are given, along with peace of mind and heart. There are other paths to God-knowledge, of course, but this is one path easily available to many and the chief reason for the worldwide interest and enduring value placed on meditation. It is a tool for learning spiritual psychology, a technique for expanding consciousness.

The highest development in meditation, regardless of the "school" or "path," brings technique and daily life together. When learning and living are integrated in spontaneous practice moment to moment, the meditator becomes what has been called "meditation in action." Meditation is no longer just a tool or device or mental exercise, no longer just a "visit" to that state in which the larger sense of self-as-cosmos emerges. The gains from meditation become integrated in a manner of living which is best described as enlightenment. The meditator has so completely mastered the lessons of meditation that his entire life is a demonstration of the higher consciousness which can be experienced if sincerely sought.

People such as that have always been recognized through the ages as special persons for whom attention and reverence is proper. For them the alteration of consciousness called mediation has led to a transformation of consciousness. Changing consciousness changes thought, changing thought changes behavior, and changing behavior changes society. Thus, the changed ones live as inspiring examples for others who are on their way to personal transformation and who seek a viable, benign means of effecting planetary transformation.

That is the fullest development of meditation. Personal evolution become social revolution. By changing yourself, you help to change the world. That is the value of meditation.

CHAPTER 10

A CHRISTIAN MANTRA FOR MEDITATION

This is drawn from *A Practical Guide to Death & Dying*, published in 1980 by Quest Books and now available from Paraview Press/Cosimo Books. It offers practical instruction for beginning to meditate by using a mantra drawn from the Christian tradition.

Meditation is a means of personal and transpersonal growth. It is a time-honored technique—probably humanity's oldest spiritual discipline—for helping people release their potential for expanded consciousness and fuller living. Also a technique for assisting in the enlightenment process of directly knowing God or ultimate reality, meditation appears in some form in nearly every major religious tradition. The entranced yogi in a lotus posture, the Zen Buddhist sitting in zazen, the Christian contemplative kneeling in adoration of Jesus, the Sufi dervish whirling in an ecstasy-inducing state—all can be properly described as practicing meditation. Although the cultural or religious trappings may vary, meditation's core experience is an altered state of consciousness in which your ordinary sense of "I"—the ego—is diminished, while a larger sense of self-existence-merged-with-the-cosmos comes into awareness.

When your self-centered consciousness is dissolved, your true identity shines through. This is enlightenment, cosmic consciousness union with God. The experience is transforming. Your life changes because you realize the essential truth of what spiritual teachers, sages and saints have said: Death as nonexistence is an illusion, there is nothing to fear, and it is only your petty little ego which generates the fear, along with the sorrow, greed, jealously, pride, lust and all the other sins, vices and unfulfilling desires which make life miserable for you and for others. Fear of death is the ego's "recoil from infinity." Fear of death is ultimately fear of enlightenment—that is, fear of living as one with the cosmos, fear of becoming an infinity-based personality.

The following meditation exercise can be quite helpful to the transformation. It's one I've devised, based on the suggestion of a friend. I've adopted it from Transcendental Meditation, which is a form of yogic meditation and uses a mantra or special sound which is mentally repeated over and over. The TM mantras are Sanskrit words, but you will use an English word: *Thine*. You should think of it as the condensed meaning of the line from the Lord's Prayer, "Thy will be done." In other words, you will be repeating to yourself a meaningful sound which essentially says, "Thy will be done, O God—not mine." The point of this mantra is to consciously begin "letting go and letting God," reducing the selfish tendency we all have to assert our little ego into the center ring and try to run the whole show. Death, of course, is the ultimate threat to the ego and insofar as we identify ourselves with the ego, we fear death, we try to deny it through self-glorifying activities, we try to avoid it through elaborate "security" measures.

None of that works, though. The only sane alternative is to confront it. In doing so, we find, paradoxically, that as we become less and less self-centered, more and more cosmically centered, death becomes less and less frightful. As the constricted consciousness of ego opens up, death is seen to be threatening only to the illusion which we mistook to be our real self. The fear often felt by people when deep in meditation is the ego's response to the perception that it is being "swallowed by infinity." Which is precisely the case! But from the point of self-transcendence, that is exactly what needs to be done.

Meditation, as I've said, eliminates the obstacles of mind which prevent clarity of consciousness and full perception of reality. Mindfulness, not mindlessness, is the mark of proper meditation. You expand awareness, not eliminate it. You extinguish egotism, revealing your true self which is one with God and is therefore deathless.

Before giving you instructions, I must make two brief comments about when it's best *not* to meditate. First, do not meditate after a meal because most likely you'll only fall asleep. Your body has mobilized itself to digest food, which reduces blood flow to the brain. Less oxygen is passing through and consequently you get that sleepy feeling. Wait an hour or so to avoid dozing off. Second, don't try to meditate just before going to sleep. You may stay up half the night because meditation can leave you feeling wide awake and charged with energy.

To do this meditation, sit down on a chair or couch. Sit up straight but not rigid. As you meditate you may find that you relax so much that you slump over to one side, or you head may nod down to your chest. That's okay, but if you become aware of this happening while you meditate, you should gently bring yourself back to the upright position.

Your hands can be folded or resting in your lap—whatever feels comfortable to you. Loosen all wearing apparel which feels tight or binding so that blood circulation and breathing are unrestricted. Remove distracting items such as wallets and pocket change. Breathe through your nose unless there is compelling reason not to. Keep your feet flat on the floor, although if your legs relax and fall to the side, that's also okay. Again, when you become aware of it, gently bring them back to an upright but comfortable position.

Choose a place indoors where the light is not too bright and the noise level is low. Take the telephone off the hook or silence your cell phone and make sure you're not going to be disturbed for half an hour. Later on, with experience, you may choose to meditate outside.

You're going to meditate for fifteen to twenty minutes. Since meditation tends to take you away from a time-keeping frame of mind, you should have a watch or clock arranged in such a way that you can easily see it without having to change your position. Then you can open your eyes slightly to see how long it's been. Don't be surprised if you think it's only been three or four minutes and then open your eyes to find that it's been fifteen. Meditation works that way. (With just a little practice you'll develop a pretty good sense of when to end your meditation, and the watch or clock won't be necessary any longer.)

To begin, settle yourself comfortably into the meditating position which suits you. Sit quietly with your eyes open for a few moments without trying to think, and then close your eyes. For perhaps a minute just sit quietly without attempting to say the mantra. Most people normally breathe at a rate of about sixteen breaths per minute, so use your breathing as a guide to time yourself. Just sit there and count sixteen breaths while you let your mind and nervous system settle down. Then silently say to yourself, "Thine." You can say it at whatever speed you want and you will probably find that you experiment a bit. Try coordinating it with your breathing and say "Thine" as you breathe out. Just keep saying "Thine" silently in your mind over and over. If your attention wanders away from saying your mantra—which it's almost certain to do—that's all right. That's part of the process of learning meditation. But as soon as you become aware that you have stopped saying your mantra, you should gently and effortlessly come back to it. Start repeating "Thine, Thine, Thine."

During the time your attention is off the mantra, all sorts of interesting thoughts, feelings and images may come into your field of awareness. That's all right, too. Don't try to stop them forcefully. Carefully but casually observe them, without becoming entangled in them or attached to them. You may start watching an adventuresome drama starring yourself, or recalling various real-life experiences, or pondering some problematic situation. Often the imagery of your meditation will be very insightful, and you'll recall it afterward. Whatever it may be, however, when you become aware that you're not saying the mantra, gently let those thoughts go and begin to repeat the mantra again.

When you've decided to end your meditation, simply stop saying the mantra and sit quietly for about two minutes with your eyes closed. Let your physical senses gradually restore themselves. Then slowly begin to open your eyes. Take the full two minutes to do so, counting breaths if necessary to time it. That serves the purpose of avoiding shock to your nervous system which is now in a very quiet and sensitized condition.

After the two minutes of "rising to the surface," your eyes will be fully open and you'll be completely aware of your environment. You may have moved your body, hands or legs somewhat during meditation—it's perfectly okay to do so in this exercise—but you will probably now find yourself in a position that you've been holding in a relaxed way for five or ten minutes, perhaps longer.

Stretch your arms, rub your face and eyes, and get yourself into motion. You'll feel like you are waking up after a good night's sleep, and maybe you'll yawn or heave a deep sign. But within a few minutes you'll probably feel wide awake and full of energy.

If you wish to modify this meditation with a mantra of your own choosing, feel free to do so.

When the student is ready the teacher will appear—in some form, be it a person, a book or an experience. The important thing is to seek.

For in the stillness of meditation this can be direct insight into the nature of yourself—an insight which carries conviction beyond all intellectual argument and emotional unburdening. The eternal and immortal creation, from which we are inseparable in its fulness, is our true identity. Even more than that, we are one with the Source of all creation. We are all creation and the Creator, now and forever. Only the ego fears death. But the ego is a false image of ourself based on attachment to a perishable body. We wrongly and unconsciously identify with this image, and thus *cause ourselves* to suffer. Meditation is the time-honored means for seeing through the illusion which generates suffering and fear of death

CHAPTER 11

MYSTICISM AND MORALITY

T his was a letter to an author of a book about mystical sex. I have
expanded it for this book.

Dear L:

Mysticism is not a single experience or state, nor is there only one
"brand" of mysticism. You say that mysticism celebrates the senses.
I say that *some* forms and schools of mysticism do; others don't.
The asceticism of some lines of yoga, for example, seeks only to
mortify the senses on the assumption that the senses bind us to
illusion, *maya*. Furthermore, even in mystical traditions which are
not world-denying, there is recognition of beginning, intermediate
and final states of mystical experience, as in the distinction among
savikalpa samadhi, nirvikalpa samadhi and sahaj samadhi. Some
religions have been founded upon beginning, intermediate and final
forms of mystical apprehension. So some commentators—myself
included—say there are higher and lower forms of mysticism. It's not
that the lower are wrong; they're just lower, which means incomplete
or less than final, or junior rather than senior. The highest form is
that which sees God in all things and all things in God, including
the physical realm. No aspect of creation is rejected; rather, all is

transformed through the redeeming experience of seeing everything as an expression of the Divine.

"Seeing God in all things" is a way of describing the first great aspect of the Whole, which is Being. "Seeing all things in God" is a way of describing the second great aspect of the Whole, which is Becoming. Understanding both is the noetic aspect of enlightenment. Living both is the behavioral aspect of enlightenment.

Conventional religion tends to be concerned with Being. Conventional morality tends to be concerned with Becoming.

Both religion and morality are therefore derivatives of mystical experience. (Yes, there are moral or ethical systems designed on the basis of reason and logic, as in humanism or ethical culture, but these are modern developments, and don't bear on this aspect of my comments.) In practice, institutional religions have a mixture of both mysticism and morality because the founders—who were great mystics—recognized through direct apprehension that there is a moral structure to the universe. There are moral absolutes to be realized.

Morality and Ultimate Reality

To put it another way, morality is inherent in the nature of Being, and enlightened living—or an aspiration to that state—requires a person to conduct his or her life in accord with the nature of ultimate reality. Why is it inherent? Ultimate reality is God, plain and simple. Human apprehension of God identifies various qualities, aspects and attributes of the nature of God—for example, love, generosity, splendor, power, justice, goodness, patience. Many of those qualities, aspects and attributes are articulated at the human level as virtues.

What is a virtue and why should humans strive to be virtuous? A virtue is a reflection of the character of God, and we should strive to be virtuous—that is, to be moral and of good character—because it expresses God more fully in our lives. The opposite of virtue is vice or immorality, which is lack of godliness in one or another aspect of our living. If the purpose of human life is to grow to godhood—which is what mysticism asserts—then virtuous living is the foundation for that process because it begins to inculcate godly qualities in us. As Henry

Bayman, author of *The Station of No Station* (which is a study of Islamic Sufism) says, "To put it in a nutshell: no ethics, no enlightenment."

Thus, theoretically speaking, morality is not in conflict with mysticism, nor is religion. For example, the Golden Rule as a guide to religio-moral conduct is found in all the major religions of the world. It is simply a prescription for obtaining the best or most satisfying interpersonal relations and it is based on recognition of God's love as the fundamental reality governing and attracting all life.

The problem with implementing the Golden Rule is that not everyone who belongs to a religion or who nominally adheres to a moral system has the mystical understanding which the founder had and therefore lacks the noetic perspective to conduct himself or herself in accord with the insights codified in religion and morality. St. Augustine boiled it all down to "Love, and do as thou wilt." That's a lovely expression of mysticism in action by a highly spiritual person, but it's not likely to make great headway among mafioso, teenage gangs, terrorists, etc. Aleister Crowley went further overboard by saying, "Do as thou wilt shall be the whole of the law." Such license simply doesn't work, as Crowley's own life sadly attests.

Thus it is no coincidence that all the world's major religions and sacred traditions have moral codes which are regarded as integral to them. Judeo-Christianity has the Ten Commandments, yoga has its Yamas and Niyamas, Buddhism has its Right Actions, Islam has its Sharia, and so forth. These moral codes are the foundation for higher human development in those traditions, and without a deep internalization of them, the spiritual aspirant can get lost in the labyrinth of inner space. Gopi Krishna used to tell me that they are so intrinsic to the process of awakening kundalini properly and safely that they constitute nature's safeguard against enlightenment for someone who is not morally prepared and who otherwise might become an evil genius.

Exoteric vs. Esoteric Religion

So when you describe religion as you do and when you say "the average person believes that..." you are criticizing the exoteric forms of religion and morality, not the esoteric. You can't divorce morality from any of the great religions because morality is integral to the founder's experience of understanding. Karma, for example, is fundamental to Hinduism and Buddhism, and was a part of the world-view of Jesus (although its corollary, reincarnation, has been expunged from Christianity). Karma is essentially a way of saying the universe is fundamentally moral and works for justice in our lives. The fact that this is not understood or is misunderstood or is foolishly distorted into a thousand competing doctrines and denominations is no critique of the esoteric form of religion—only of human failings.

I therefore disagree with you when you say "mysticism is not simply a more true or sublime form of popular religion." Mysticism is precisely that. Mysticism is a more true or sublime form of popular religion. Most of the forms which mystical experience eventually ends up producing—popular religions—are, objectively speaking, degenerate forms or pale reflections of mystical experience. Yet even in their most grotesque distortions they retain seeds of ultimate truth. That truth is common to the major religions and has been rediscovered time after time by people who've had the courage to follow their heart outside the pale of approved behavior and belief into the Divine Domain. (Aldous Huxley called that truth "the perennial philosophy." You should read his excellent book of the same title.) Such people often return to the world and to their religious institutions, where they work selflessly for people's salvation/enlightenment by encouraging them to undertake their own mystical awakening and thereby discover through personal experience the transcendent unity of religions and the sisterhood/brotherhood of all people.

The Two Commonalities of Major Religions

In the course of rediscovering the perennial philosophy or the primordial tradition or the timeless wisdom, mystics have not ignored morality and, as I said, it is no accident that the Golden Rule is found in one form or another in all the great religions. In fact, as I view things, there are two prime commonalities in the major religions. First, they all have an injunction about how people should behave in order to get along best with one another (which in its simplest form is a variant of the Golden Rule). Second, they all have a practice for God-realization (which, admittedly, is all but lost in the exoteric dimension and is found largely in the small communities of esotericism which adhere to the body of the religion, such as Kabbalah in Judaism, Sufism in Islam and Hesychasm in Christianity). Both of these prime commonalities flow directly from mystic realization.

Now, it is true that no amount of morality will produce mystical experience. In that sense, morality is indeed "outside" mysticism. However, it is outside only because it is the foundation, not the completion, of mystical practice. It is not outside the mystical experience per se. Your critique of morality on the basis of comparative anthropology and linguistic analysis doesn't deal with the heart of the matter, as I see it. What you describe as "good/virtuous/moral" is inherent in the course of completing mystical realization or self-transcendence, not external to it. The spiritual voyager goes from atonement to at-one-ment; s/he goes from a sense of sinfulness, guilt and unworthiness arising from ego-domination to a sense of oneness with all creation arising from ego-transcendence.

But on the path of higher human development, you must first have an ego before you can transcend the ego. At the ego-stage of understanding, we come to recognize "higher" authority which gives us guidance for attaining enlightenment; some of that guidance may appear as moral commandments because there is need for correcting our wrongful behavior: atonement. (All sacred traditions have commandments or ethical rules of behavior. They are the starting point for conscious, responsible conduct on the spiritual path.) Beyond ego, we recognize ourselves as the source of moral authority, but the "self" in "ourselves" is not the ego-self; it is God/Dharma/Tao/Allah, etc. We are one with that: at-one-ment.

If there is such a thing at all as mysticism, it can only be because there is such a thing as human nature and human potential. That being so, morality or virtuous behavior is also inherent in the process of realizing one's ultimate nature and will be discovered to be alike in all times and cultures—for the simple reason that God is one. God is the supreme reality behind everything! So it is no accident or coincidence that every society and every religion not only recognizes morality and has moral codes, but also has deep agreement on the essentials of morality (virtues)—such as truthfulness and compassion—which are universally recognized as ideals for higher human development. "In essentials, unity; in nonessentials, liberty; in all things, charity." (Thank you for that pithy wisdom, William Penn.)

The Goal of Mysticism

Noetically speaking, there is a profound difference between morality and mysticism. Morality is the foundation for mystical ascent; without a solid moral foundation, the person who has a mystical experience will at least be unguided and confused, and may even become unhinged (a lá kundalini-gone-astray). Mysticism is the completion of a process which begins with morality, but they're quite different. Morality can produce piety, but in and of itself, cannot produce enlightenment. A person must explore the depths of inner space for that, and morality alone does not suffice for the job. You probably know lots of moral people who don't have the slightest clue about mystical experience.

Morality begins the transformation of consciousness; mysticism completes it. Morality is the launch pad, mysticism is the spacecraft and enlightenment is the landing site after the difficult journey through inner space. Morality alone will not produce a compassionate person; it will only restrain him from being a brutal one. Compassion, unconditional love, generosity and other qualities of the enlightened sages arise from experience which goes beyond morality into mysticism. In that experience, they perceive directly that they are one with all others; they perceive directly how suffering arises and how that leads to all the egoic defenses which produce man's inhumanity to man. Morality places restraints on behavior; mysticism removes restraints on understanding. Morality tells you abstractly that we are all one; mysticism demonstrates it directly.

The bottom line is: I agree that the goal of mysticism is not to be good/virtuous/moral but to attain self-transcendence. However, mysticism nevertheless recognizes that good/virtuous/moral conduct is necessary for attaining the goal of mysticism and that the true nature of "self" includes all others. That quite naturally leads to the necessity for behavior codes to facilitate best relations with those others, as well as insight into how best to do that, i.e., morality. It is possible to attain beginning and intermediate mystical experiences yet be abjectly ignorant of moral values or indifferent to them. Aleister Crowley would be an example of that, I suppose; so would Hitler, as I point out in *Kundalini, Evolution and Enlightenment*. It is also possible to be genuinely moral, yet be abjectly ignorant of our human potential for self-transcendence; many pious fundamentalists of various religions are examples of that. Neither condition is wrong in itself—they're merely partial or incomplete. Higher human development is a process which requires a moral foundation from which to ascend into metaphysical realms, and mystical experience by which to complete it. The result is enlightenment or God-realization and its expression throughout all aspects of your life.

Regards,
John

CHAPTER 12

MEDITATION AND HIGHER HUMAN DEVELOPMENT — A LOOK AT THE BIG PICTURE

This was an extemporaneous talk given at a church in Connecticut in 1994 to a group exploring spiritual development. I have transcribed a tape recording of it and expanded it slightly for publication.

Meditation is one of the time-honored tools we have for unfolding our potential to live, in the words of Jesus, "as gods." That is, we human beings have a profound potential for growth to higher consciousness and a higher state of being. Meditation is one of the techniques for assisting and accelerating that process. It has developed worldwide and is used worldwide.

I want to talk about meditation this evening in context of "the big picture." The goal of life is enlightenment. Well, what is enlightenment? I'll speak about that, but first I want to quote a wonderful little maxim by Thaddeus Golas, author of *The Lazy Man's Guide to Enlightenment*. He says, "Enlightenment doesn't care how you get there." That's so true! Attaining enlightenment need not involve meditation at all in the sense of practicing a formal technique. However, insofar as meditation is a time-honored practice recommended by all sacred traditions, it is a means of unfolding our potential through all the levels of our being—and doing that in a safe, efficient manner.

My friend Bo Lozoff, founder of the Human Kindness Foundation in Durham, North Carolina, used to tell a story which is very pertinent here. The story is about a rabbi who would say, "Enlightenment is not earned—it's an accident." One of the rabbi's students asked, "Since it's an accident, why do you make me spend so much time in prayer and meditation?" The rabbi replied, "To be as accident-prone as possible."

Sacred traditions around the world say that, in general, there are three levels of reality on which we exist simultaneously: the physical, the mental and the spiritual. That's a simple way of classifying or categorizing the aspects of our nature which are recognized in the worldviews of all sacred traditions. All that can be conceptualized as levels of existence or levels of being. Meditation enables us to grow from the lowest level—the physical—through the mental and spiritual levels of our being to a sense of realization of our oneness with the divine, the source of all those levels, the source of all being. That, paradoxically, turns out to be who we have been all along, who we always are, and who we shall be forever, beyond all individuality and beyond all temporal forms we inhabit. In other words, our ultimate identity, our true self is none other than one with the source of all creation. We are temporarily inhabiting the limited form of a body, but we need not identify with that form in the sense of constricting our consciousness to think we are only that. Meditation is a way of transcending those boundaries of consciousness which lead to a false identity, a false sense of self.

Now, as we ascend in consciousness through the levels of being which constitute the totality of reality, there's also a movement which we can conceive of as having a horizontal direction, in contrast to the vertical direction—and that's time. So as we develop, we move forward in time to discover what is essentially our timeless self above and beyond all the partial identities we may have. Above and below and beyond and within all the levels of being, there is that source of being—the source of all creation which sustains all creation, moment to moment to moment, even as it's sustaining you and me at this very instant. If it were to withdraw that power for even a nanosecond, the whole universe would vanish—utterly annihilated. There would just be nothing. No thing. Nothing. Can you comprehend that?

The Yogic Stages of Life

Something is sustaining and enfolding the universe, including us, and meditation helps us to sense, recognize, become aware of that universal power and presence which is none other than the center of our own being as well. Our essence is one with the essence of all creation. In the language of Hinduism, the Atman—the deepest center of the self—is one with the Brahman, the deepest center of all creation. The ancient yogis developed a schema of higher human development which divided the life cycle into four major periods, each of about 25 years. In other words, they conceived of a typical lifetime as being about 100 years long, with four major stages of growth or development which people went through—or could go through—in that lifetime.

The first twenty-five years or so is the stage of the *brahmacharya*. That is the stage of the student. It's the child growing up, going through adolescence and becoming a man or woman, becoming a citizen of his or her community, having the schooling experience, learning the ways of culture, and becoming a functional person able to go out into the world on his or her own.

The second stage—another 25 years or so, bringing you to about mid-life—is the stage of the householder. That is when the mature person—physically mature as an adult, that is—typically marries, has children, gets involved in all the civic responsibilities which go with being a member of a society, performs his or her job, raises a family and then sees the children go off into the world at toward the end of that second stage of a person's life.

That brings the person to the third stage of life which, in the traditional view of the yogis, is a stage of attending to one's own spiritual growth, one's spiritual needs, in a very focused, concentrated way. This is the stage of being a forest yogi. That is to say, one has finished up with householder responsibilities and is then free to go, free to leave on a spiritual journey to find a deeper sense of self—in short, to attain enlightenment. Now, that doesn't mean one has to leave one's spouse. It's said in ancient scriptures that husband and wife could, and sometimes did, go off together. However, the point is, they didn't take the kids, they didn't have the household and community responsibilities. They didn't worry about PTA and Rotary Club duties, shopping lists, lawn mowing and all the rest of that. They leave all that behind. In a sense, they leave the world and go on retreat. However, it's a strategic retreat in order to advance. In the yogic scheme of things, that stage is when higher human development begins—development beyond ego. Again, it is about 25 years, at the end of which, theoretically speaking, one attains enlightenment.

Well, what do you do when you're enlightened? That's when the fourth stage of human life begins in the yogic scheme of things. That is the stage in which you re-enter the marketplace, the community, as a teacher or guru, as one who knows, realizes, is awakened, understands the nature of Ultimate Reality and can help others find their way to a realization of their own deepest nature.

At the end of the fourth stage of human development, the yogi "casts off the body" and then continues his or her spiritual practice in a noncorporeal form until such time as the Lords of Karma—as the mysterious process of postmortem survival and rebirth is called—reincarnate him or he chooses to take on another form of physical existence on this planet, perhaps, or on another planet or another plane of existence altogether. Or perhaps like Buddha, he embraces unconditional *mahasamadhi*—that is, totally vanishes out of space-time altogether, leaving not a trace behind. Not a physical, not a mental, not even a spiritual trace of the psychophysical organism. That, in my view, is what Jesus accomplished at the end of the 40 days after his resurrection. That is when he ascended into heaven and, as the Gospel of John puts it, resumed the glory he shared with the Father before creation.

Stages of Development and Planes of Being

However, that's another story, which I cover in my book *The Meeting of Science and Spirit*. (Also see Chapter 9.) I'm just trying to lay out here in very broad terms the notion that over the course of a lifetime there are stages of development and those stages can be correlated with levels of being, or planes of reality, if you will. In the first stage, the child is not very spiritually aware. A child may have very rich, healthy spiritual instincts, but don't ask it to get into any heavy philosophy or metaphysics. It's not yet capable of intellectually describing the sort of things I'm talking about right now because it hasn't gone that far into the mental plane. Incidentally, when I say "mental," I mean both intellectual and emotional.

So, as one journeys forward in time, one is also exploring higher and higher levels of being. One is becoming aware of, and in control of, those unfolding aspects of one's nature which are not immediately obvious or present as an infant or as a child or as a student. So by the end of the second stage of life, the householder stage, one should theoretically be in control of the physical and the mental planes—that is, have the knowledge of and the ability to work appropriately, even wisely, with the full range of one's physical and intellectual-rational capacities. And to be aware, of course, that there are still higher levels to explore, with their innate qualities and faculties which will unfold in you as you enter those higher planes of being and begin to master them.

So the enlightened person is one who is really a master of consciousness. He or she has a profound understanding of the nature of human beings, including himself or herself, but is not exclusively identified with any part of that. Rather, the sense of identity, the supreme identity we all have, is one which embraces it all yet transcends it all—utterly, totally, absolutely transcends the entire space-time framework of the cosmos. We exist in time but we are not limited by time in our essence, in our ultimate nature.

A Cosmic Mudra

Now, let me bring all that back to meditation for a moment with a consideration of a very simple hand gesture which is sometimes used in meditation. As I sit in meditation, or if I'm doing hatha yoga, laying on the floor in the corpse pose with my arms out, my fingers just naturally assume this position, this hand gesture, this mudra, as certain hand gestures are called in the yogic tradition (and Buddhist tradition also since Buddha began his spiritual life as a forest yogi in India). And, although I've not read about this in any book, it seems to me that there is an understanding—an interpretation, at least—which symbolizes all which I've just said to you about planes of being and stages of development. [1] Look at that gesture. Look at that hand posture. If I were sitting in meditation, my hands would be resting comfortably on my thighs. Sometimes I might use the Zen hand-position, but I simply find it most comfortable to sit like this, with my thumb and forefinger forming a circle, surmounting the other three fingers, which are slightly curled but completely relaxed.

Now think about it. I've just said that all sacred traditions recognize three great realms of being which constitute our embodied nature: the physical, the mental and the spiritual. However, those traditions also say that our true identity, who we ultimately are, is not to be located in any one of those realms, and is not to be bound by any one of those realms—or even by all of them together. The physical, mental and spiritual can be thought of as constituting the total universe, the entire cosmos. However, if you identify yourself exclusively with any part of that or even with all of it, you have created a limit on your consciousness—a boundary and a false sense of identity based on it. Because, as I said earlier, who you ultimately are is the source of all creation. That source includes all creation yet infinitely transcends all creation. Yes, we temporarily inhabit these physical bodies with their mental and spiritual qualities, and they are an expression of God, a form of God. However, your body is going to get old and decay and die some day and pass away. What happens to you then? Who are you then?

Well, the evidence of parapsychology is validating what ancient traditions have said: "Yes, there is a noncorporeal, nonphysical part of us which continues with postmortem existence." Since it's beyond or above the physical, it's *meta*physical and traditionally is called "soul." You temporarily experience that condition in out-of-body states; you temporarily experience it in near-death experiences; you temporarily experience it in high meditative states. However, even that is not who you ultimately are. You are not even ultimately a soul. That is to say, even souls are not eternal.

Now, that phrase "the eternal soul" is very widely used and I'm not knocking it. We can agree to use certain conventional phrases for the sake of communication, but considered in its widest and deepest aspect, even souls are not eternal. Everything which is made, everything which is formed, anything which is less than the formless and the timeless is therefore not eternal and will eventually grow old, decay and dissolve back into the source of all creation. All compound things decay, Buddha said. Even souls are not eternal; they have their period of growth and development, however vast it may seem to be. However, enlightenment, self-realization or God-realization means transcending even a sense of identity as a soul and recognizing your prior oneness with the source of all souls. It's an attainment which is a nonattainment. It's a discovery which is a remembrance. And in this mudra, it is indicated by the circle—which is the most ancient symbol of infinity—formed by the thumb and the forefinger.

It's important to recognize that in this gesture the circle sits atop the three fingers. That is to say, it is senior to the junior levels represented by the three other fingers. So this simple, natural, easy gesture of your hands can be a focus for your own meditations in the search for self, true self. It can be a guide to reality—a blueprint of reality, if you will. Reality is not just the physical level—I think we are all agreed on that. However, I'm also saying it is not just the mental or the spiritual level, or even all of them combined. Reality includes all those levels but is not limited to them or by them. That's because Reality is God, and God infinitely transcends the cosmos, even while including the cosmos.

Now, this word "spirit," I should say in a kind of aside, can be used in different ways. Some people may use it as a synonym for God. They say Spirit or Spirit-in-Action. I am not using it that way at the moment. I'm saying it represents a vast domain or realm or kingdom within the total constitution of the cosmos. In this three-part schema of manifest reality, it is the most senior level of being, the top rung of the ladder. In the terminology of the yogic tradition it is called the "causal level." That is, it is the highest level of manifest reality, at which point things come into being, into existence. They become manifest and act as a cause of other events farther down the ladder, farther down the great chain of being, so to speak, at lower levels. It is the soul level.

However, God, the source of the entire universe, infinitely and absolutely transcends even that high level, that high plane of existence because God is also unmanifest reality.

You can personally experience the nature of the causal plane, and some of you may have had the experience of getting spaced out on high inner planes. The nature of the plane which I'm referring to as spirit is extremely subtle. It's also very attractive. That is as it should be; it acts, as we ascend in consciousness, to call us "home." It's an attractor. However, we can get "stuck" at any of the levels of manifest reality, and if we get stuck at the causal level, it's just another form of addiction, just another form of attachment. In this case, it's attachment to bliss, which is why some meditators are called bliss ninnies. They're always blissing out, but it's only closed-eyes bliss. It's only based on sensory withdrawal, aversion to the material world and to action in society. It's not the open-eyed bliss of one who sees the world—indeed, the whole cosmos—as a form of God. That person is as comfortable and capable of working with the dregs of humanity as he or she is with spiritually inclined people. He or she is a mystic of the marketplace.

Stress Management vs. Stress Elimination

To translate all this into contemporary terms, let's consider the subject of stress. It's wonderful that western medicine is now aware of stress and its effects. It's wonderful that there's a lot of talk about managing stress and about meditation's effectiveness as a means of managing stress. That's all very, very true. However, the stress which science is talking about exists at, and is recognized at, or is measured at the physical level. You can hook up all sorts of instruments and measure the tension of a muscle or the firing rate of a neuron or something on that order. However, those are only physiological manifestations—physical expressions—of something which originates at a higher level, at the mental level or perhaps even at the spiritual level, and science is not yet capable of measuring anything like that. Your own subjective experience probably tells you without a doubt that there are emotional and what we can call spiritual causes of stress in people. So at the physical level, while it is good to manage stress—and meditation can be useful for that—it's not the same thing as eliminating stress.

How do we eliminate stress? Before we can answer that, we really should ask: What is stress in the first place? My answer is this: Stress is not something which happens to us because of some external factor, some external cause. Stress is discomfort caused by our own response to whatever happens. If our response is based on fear or anxiety or worry, then it gets expressed in our bodies as muscle tension, as headaches, as facial tics, as overproduction of gastrointestinal juice which gives us upset stomach, heartburn, ulcers—the whole range of the physical signs of stress.

Now, we can manage that to a great extent, but those are effects, not causes. To eliminate the cause of stress, we need to do more than take medications or biofeedback training or something like that. We need to look deeply within ourselves to see who or what it is which fears or is anxious or angry or depressed in the first place. We need to look deeply within ourselves to see who produces that reaction which ultimately manifests as tension or stress or psychogenic illness. Meditation can take us safely and consciously into the realm at which stress arises and the stress reaction begins—at the mental and the spiritual levels—and actually eliminate the stress reaction, leaving only peace of mind, equanimity, tranquility, serenity.

The yogic tradition has a saying which I regard as extremely profound: "Wherever there is Other, there is fear." By that is meant, wherever one's sense of self as the Whole is not fully and immediately present, precisely *there* exists a boundary in consciousness. Precisely *there* exists a limitation in the sense of who or what you conceive yourself to be. That boundary, that limitation in your own consciousness, is self-created. It's important to recognize that a self-created boundary says, "Whatever is outside this boundary is threatening to me" because I regard it as not-me. I regard it as Other. It's something I don't really know and recognize as familiar, like my own face. Not only do I not know it, I don't trust it, I don't feel comfortable with it, I don't feel at home with it. It upsets me, it puts me on edge, it keeps me in a state of constant expectation of danger, of attack. It keeps me, to one degree or another, guarded and in a chronic state of fear.

The Recovery of Unconditional Happiness

Well, that's where meditation can help us. It can help us to see through the illusion of separateness, that false identity which we developed thinking we are only this or only that—some partial sense of relatedness to the whole. If enlightenment can be said to be anything at all, it is happiness—unbound, unbroken, unconditional happiness. In the yogic tradition, the name of every swami—that is, a person who puts on the orange robe and takes holy orders in the yogic tradition—ends with the word "ananda," which is Sanskrit for "bliss." It means the unbroken happiness which is experienced by enlightened, self-realized beings. Now, that's not to say every monk or yogi whose name ends in -ananda is an enlightened being with unbroken happiness, but the suffix is meant for them as a reminder, if you will, or as an image of the goal they strive for in their spiritual endeavors.

How can anyone be totally happy if there's anything which seems to be outside himself or herself and which is to any degree whatsoever foreign or threatening? That person can't be totally happy. He or she always has to be somewhat on guard, somewhat contracted into an inner stance of suspicion, distrust, uneasiness. So happiness, in the sense of an unbroken, abiding inner peace and comfort and ease with being in the world—not dis-ease, but only ease—arises from discovering your true self. Happiness is finding the supreme identity, who you are already but simply have not realized in your ordinary waking awareness.

Meditation can help you penetrate through to those higher and higher levels of being. By the way, in those levels there are all sorts of potential traps and byways and dysfunctions and mental disorders such as I mentioned about bliss—as well as new faculties and new understandings. Getting subtly puffed up with false pride about being apparently humble is an example. Meditation can help you to find your way safely through those planes to that condition called enlightenment. That is a condition which understands that all of creation, all of manifest reality is not who you ultimately are. You include all that but you transcend all that because you are, in the final sense, one with the source of all that. The whole universe could in theory be annihilated—just utterly vanish. In fact, some myths of creation say precisely that has happened many times. If the whole cosmos disappeared, who would you be then? The answer enlightenment gives is: None other than who you are already in the sense of "whatever it is which produced you and all others as living beings here on the physical plane." You and I are all one from the point of view of that supreme identity. That unity-in-diversity, that One-in-all is what meditation can help us to discover experientially, beyond mere verbal descriptions such as I'm giving you now.

In discovering that supreme identity, in realizing ourselves as one with God, our existence becomes ultimately meaningful and infinitely blissful because we are liberated and infinitely free—free from delusion, free from attachments, free from self-ignorance. There may be troubles and tribulations and discomforts in your life. You may have circumstances which are perplexing or painful in an outward sense, but they don't bother you in the center of your being—where you really live. They're just sort of happening around the edges, if you will. That doesn't mean you ignore them or disdain them. It just means that—hey, they're human circumstances. They've happened to other people. They can happen to me. They come and they go, just as people come and go. You deal with them intelligently, lovingly. But they're not permanent. Will they matter to you when you're dead? Who were you before you were in this body? What will you be after you no longer have this body?

Meditation can help you to see the vast expanse of time in which this evolutionary journey we're all on is operating. Not just the human journey but also the universe's journey. From the beginning of the universe there has been an evolutionary development of matter out of nothingness and then matter building up in more complex forms— stellar sequences which produce galaxies, and galaxies which produce planetary systems, and planetary systems which produce simple one-celled organisms, and one-celled organisms which grow into more complex forms, into—here on Planet Earth—the fishes, which evolve into amphibians, from which a few members evolve still further into the mammals, from which arise protohumans. Then, about six million years ago, some of our progenitors running around the plains of Africa said, "Hey! I've got an idea. I think I'll become a human!" Well, perhaps not quite like that. However it happened, six million years later we find ourselves sitting in a room in St. John's Episcopal Church in Waterbury, Connecticut, contemplating the cosmic processes operating through vast expanses of time and space which have led us to come together for this moment.

Beholding the Mystery of Creation

It is awesome. It is awful—full of awe. It fills one with awe to behold the mystery of creation and to recognize that you are one with it, even as it seems in its majesty and grandeur and incomprehensibility to be beyond any effort we can make to put it into words and express it in some neat little formula. For me, at least, there is a mystery beyond all the circumstances which we can understand and describe, and that mystery is traditionally called God. But by whatever name that Great Mystery, that *Mysterium tremendum*, is named, it is not apart from you, it is not apart from me. Even if we can't completely *com*prehend it, we can nevertheless *ap*prehend it—apprehend it deeply. It is the very essence of us. So whenever we find ourselves suffering—that is, psychologically hurting from a sense of self-pity or false pride or alienation or loss or whatever—that's a *direct* measure of the amount of ego we have invested in this situation. That's a direct measure of the amount of limited self-sense with which we are operating in that situation. That's a direct measurement of the degree to which we're sleepwalking rather than awake, aware, conscious.

Our true self is without limitation. It is unbounded consciousness. It was before the beginning of the world; it will be after the end of the world. It was before the beginning of time; it will be after the end of time. That unbounded consciousness has been called, in the Christian tradition, the Christ Consciousness. There are names for it in other sacred traditions, such as "our Original Face," as Buddhism puts it. In the Christian tradition we see in Jesus a pattern of higher human development which we can emulate, which we can model ourselves upon. That's "the imitation of Christ." [2] Such models exist in other traditions—Buddha, for example, and Krishna. And, as I said earlier, enlightenment doesn't care how you get there. The important thing is to fix your heart on knowing God, on knowing that source of all creation, on knowing your own deepest nature, your true self.

With that stance of consciousness on your part, a loving Creator and its creation, the cosmos, will provide everything you need to nurture you every step of the way toward that wonderful recognition of "Wow, I'm at home in the universe. There's nothing here which is not a part of me, nothing I can't relate to as an aspect of my own true self." With that comes "the peace of God which passes all understanding" abiding in your heart and mind. There also arises compassion for all sentient beings, including your fellow humans who are still in darkness and struggling to find their way into the light. There also arises wisdom to help them, to guide them. The heart opens and the wisdom-eye opens. Happiness and understanding arise.

Meditation can be an important tool for attaining that condition. I don't say it is absolutely necessary as a formal practice, but it certainly is time-honored, and I recommend it highly. If you practice meditation, you might consider what I said this evening about the focus of your meditation—namely, this simple hand gesture. The physical, the mental and the spiritual constitute manifest reality, and you as a created being contain those aspects of reality. But the circle, the symbol of infinity which is senior to them, is the source from which manifest reality flows and which is also the source of your true identity. So your beingness also includes the unmanifest aspect of reality—the uncreated. That is where all worlds arise and eventually return; that is the glory of God before he said "Let there be light." And that is who you ultimately are.

[1]   Recently I learned from yogi-scholar, Georg Feuerstein, that this hand posture is called the jnana-mudra (or gyan-mudra) in the yogic tradition, symbolizing inner knowledge. *Jnana* is the Sanskrit word for transcendental knowledge; its English cognate is *gnosis*. In Feuerstein's newsletter, *Yoga World* (No. 12, January-March 2000), his associate Richard Miller elaborates in an article on mudras: "There is a beautiful tradition according to which the thumb represents Unity Consciousness or Universal Self, the index finger the individual self, the middle finger the ego, the ring finger maya or misperception, and the little finger worldly actions and reactions. As the individual self—through meditational Self-inquiry—reaches up to merge with its Source (Unity Consciousness), it moves away from the involvement

with the false sense of separation (ego), maya (misperception), and worldly actions and reactions. Perceiving the deep yearning for Self-realization, the Universal Self, with compassion and grace, reaches down and pulls the individual self into Itself, revealing Itself as Itself." (p. 5) *Yoga World*'s address is: Traditional Yoga Studies, P.O. Box 661, Eastend, Saskatchewan S0N 0T0, Canada.

[2] This statement equates Jesus with The Christ, and while that is true, it is also incomplete. As I point out in Chapter 21, "The Judeo-Christian Tradition and the New Age," in *The Meeting of Science and Spirit*, rather than saying "Jesus was the Christ," it is more accurate to say "The Christ was Jesus." That allows for other Christs, including you and me. Through modeling ourselves upon the life and teaching of Jesus, we can attain Christhood— which is precisely what Jesus wanted for people! As the noted psychic Edgar Cayce said in one of his readings, Jesus is the pattern and Christ is the power.

Here is a poem I wrote on that theme in 1970; it was published in *Science of Mind* in December 1976.

SEASON'S GREETINGS

And every day is Christmas if you listen
To the voice of God within you.
Not long ago and far away
But here and now Christ is born—
In you, in me.

And this is the miracle of incarnation—
Not that he was a man like us
But that we are gods like him,
Not that he shares our humanity
But that we share his divinity.

CHAPTER 13

PARANOIA, METANOIA AND THE AQUARIAN CONSPIRACY

There is a conspiracy which readers should know of because it is totally the opposite of alleged conspiracies by the New World Order aiming at global control and imposition of tyranny. It is called the Aquarian Conspiracy.

The name comes from a 1980 book entitled *The Aquarian Conspiracy* by Marilyn Ferguson. In it she described the consciousness movement under way, especially in America, aiming at personal and social transformation to a new world, a New Age, an Aquarian Age. The book has been in print continuously since then, and was recently supplemented by Ferguson with a second volume, *Aquarius Now: Radical Common Sense and Reclaiming Our Personal Sovereignty.*

Ferguson used the word *conspiracy* in its original sense: to breathe together. The conspiracy she described was a leaderless, unstructured process in which people all over the planet were collectively taking an "in-breath" of higher consciousness, an in-breath of Spirit. That global movement would counter and eventually conquer the sinister actions and conspiracies leading humanity toward mental and physical enslavement. It would eliminate them by transforming the consciousness of humanity, including that of the ego-driven conspirators. The satanic efforts of would-be Masters of the Universe would cease through self-understanding and transcendence of their self-centeredness. They would be turned away from enslavement and toward enlightenment, along with the rest of humanity.

In its best aspect, then, the New Age/Aquarian Age movement aims at manifesting a new mode of being—a radically transformed world inhabited by a new and higher form of humanity. That new creation would involve a social order based on love and wisdom—as envisioned by many traditions, both sacred and secular—which resolves societal disharmonies and allows people to fulfill their deepest longings for peace, truth, self-expression and freedom from the perennial problems of man's inhumanity to man.

The emergence of a higher humanity is a perennial theme in world affairs. The images drawn from this theme vary in form and purity, ranging from the inspired visions of mystics such as Sri Aurobindo to the deranged fantasies of madmen such as Adolf Hitler. The French Jesuit philosopher Pierre Teilhard de Chardin wrote of this emergence in quasi-scientific terms; yogi-scientist-philosopher Gopi Krishna addressed it more rigorously in his examination of the next evolutionary development in man via the kundalini experience; transpersonal psychologist Kenneth Ring finds evidence for it in the widespread phenomenon of the near-death experience. Occult traditions such as Theosophy, Anthroposophy, Rosicrucianism, Freemasonry, alchemy, Kabbalah and the genuine mystery schools also present the notion of the evolution of humanity to still-higher states. One of the most memorable statements about it was given by the Canadian psychiatrist, Richard M. Bucke, on the last page of his 1901 classic *Cosmic Consciousness*:

> ...just as, long ago, self-consciousness appeared in the best specimens of our ancestral race in the prime of life, and gradually became more and more universal and appeared in the individual at an earlier and earlier age, until, as we see now, it has become almost universal and appears at the average of about three years—so will Cosmic Consciousness become more and more universal earlier in the individual life until the race at large will possess this faculty. The same race and not the same; for a Cosmic Conscious race will not be the race which exists today, any more than the present race of men is the same race which existed prior to the evolution of self-consciousness. The simple truth is, that there has lived on the earth, "appearing at intervals," for thousands of years among ordinary men, the first faint beginnings of another race;

walking the earth, and breathing another air of which we know little or nothing, but which is, all the same, our spiritual life, as its absence would be our spiritual death. This new race is in the act of being born from us, and in the near future it will occupy and possess the earth.

For the majority of westerners, however, the most familiar term for this experience—the emergence of a cosmically conscious race—was given to it two millennia ago by Jesus of Nazareth.

The Son of Man

When Jesus spoke of himself, why did he principally use the term "Son of Man?" Others called him the Son of God, but Jesus most often referred to himself as the Son of Man, the offspring of humanity. Moreover, he told those around him that they would be higher than the angels and that those things which he did, they would do also, and greater (John 14:12).

The reason for this declaration by Jesus is that he was aware of himself as a finished specimen of the new humanity which is to come—the new humanity which is to inherit the Earth, establish the Kingdom, usher in the New/Aquarian Age. His mission and his teaching have at their heart the development of a new and higher state of consciousness *on a species-wide basis* rather than the sporadic basis seen earlier in history when an occasional adept or avatar such as Krishna or Buddha appeared. Jesus' unique place in history is based upon his unprecedented realization of the higher intelligence, the divinity, the Ground of Being incarnated in him—the ground which is the source of all becoming, all evolution.

Let's look at the relationship between that and paranoia because it is both a close and a profound relationship.

The Aramaic term for the Greek word "Christ" is *M'shekha*, from which we get "messiah." It is a title, not a last name, and although it is conventionally translated as "anointed," it really is better understood as "perfected" or "enlightened" or "the ideal form of humanity." Thus, Jesus was a historical person, a human being who lived two thousand years ago; but Christ, the Christos, the Messiah, is an eternal transpersonal condition of being to which *we must all someday come*. Jesus did not say that this higher state of consciousness realized in him was his alone for all time. Nor did he call us to worship him. Rather, he called us to *follow* him—to follow in his steps, to imitate him, emulate him, learn from him and his example, to live a God-centered life of selfless, compassionate service to the world *as if we were Jesus himself.* This is what is meant by the Latin phrase *imitatio Christi,* the imitation of Christ. Jesus called us to share in the new condition, to enter a new world, to be one in the higher consciousness which alone can dispel the darkness of our minds and renew our lives. He did not call us to be Christians; he called us to be Christed. In short, he aimed at *duplicating* himself by fostering the development of *many* Jesuses. He aimed, as the New Testament declares, to make all one in Christ. And who is Christ? St. Paul tells us that Christ is the Second Adam, the founder of a new race.

Metanoia and the Kingdom of Heaven

The kingdom of heaven or the kingdom of God, Jesus said, is within us and among us. Divinity is our birthright, our inheritance. To attain that, Jesus called people to awaken, to change their ways, to repent. The very first words he spoke to humanity in his public ministry were, "The time is fulfilled, and the kingdom of God is at hand; repent, and believe in the gospel" (Mark 1:14, Matthew 4:17.) This is his central teaching and commandment.

But notice the word "repent." Over the centuries it has become misunderstood and mistranslated, so that today people think it merely means feeling sorry for their sins. This is an unfortunate debasement of Jesus' teaching. The Aramaic word Jesus used is *tob,* meaning "to return" or "to flow back into God." The sense of this concept comes through best in the Greek word used to translate it. The word is *metanoia* and, like *tob,* it means something far greater than merely feeling sorry for misbehavior.

Metanoia has two etymological roots. *Meta* means "to go beyond" or "to go higher than." And *noia* comes from *nous,* meaning "mind." It is the same root from which Teilhard de Chardin developed his term *noosphere* and from which the word *noetic,* meaning "the study of consciousness," comes. It is also the term Plato used to designate the creative source of the universe prior to the Logos, the Word, which in the gospel of John refers to Jesus Christ. So the original meaning of metanoia is literally "going beyond or higher than the ordinary mental state." In modern terms, it means transcending self-centered ego and becoming God-centered, God-realized, enlightened. And when that happens on a large scale, it is, to use Ferguson's expression, "A conspiracy to establish the Aquarian Age."

Metanoia is the central experience which Jesus sought for all people. It is the heart of Jesus' life and teaching, although it is now largely absent from the institutional Christian churches. Metanoia indicates a change of mind and behavior based on radical insight into the cause and effect of one's previous actions—insight arising from entry into a condition beyond the realm of time, space and causality. Metanoia is that profound state of consciousness which mystical experience aims at—the state in which we transcend or dissolve all the barriers of ego and selfishness which separate us from God. It is the *summum bonum* of human life. It is a state of *direct knowing, unmediated perception* of our total unity with God, not through anything we have done or ever could do in a final sense (although we *must* seek to cleanse ourselves through spiritual discipline or there can be no transcendence), but simply through God's grace and unconditional love. St. Paul described it as "the renewing of your mind in Christ." Jesus said it even more simply: "I am the way" to metanoia.

In its best sense, then, metanoia means a radical conversion experience, a transformation of self-based on a new state of awareness, a new state of consciousness—higher consciousness. It means repentance in the most fundamental aspect of our existence—that of "a turning about in the deepest seat of consciousness," as Lama Govinda phrases it. That turning-about is for the purpose of re-binding or re-tieing ourselves to the divine source of our being—the source we have lost awareness of. That is what religion is all about. The word *religion* is etymologically derived from the Latin *re ligare,* meaning "to tie back, to tie again." That is true repentance—when we "get religion" in the sense of becoming aware of our inescapable ties to God, the creator, preserver and redeemer of the cosmos.

Failure to realize that is the source of all the world's troubles. But when we are rebound to God, the true meaning of sin becomes apparent. Sin means, literally, "missing the mark." "Sin is not merely misbehavior; that is only the outer aspect of it—the behavioral aspect. The inner aspect, the deeper dimension of sin, is transgression of divine law or cosmic principle. It is failure to be centered in God—to be "off target." Religion, then, is in its most fundamental and truest sense *an instrument for awakening us to the evolutionary process of growth to godhood,* which is the aim of all evolution, all growth, all cosmic

119

becoming. When we are guilty of sin, we are fundamentally missing the mark by failing to be God-conscious and all which it means for our behavior and thought.

Thus, the world is indeed in sin, but there is no remedy for it except to change consciousness. For in truth, God does not condemn us for our sins. Rather, we condemn ourselves *by* our sins. And thus forgiveness by God is not necessary; it is there always, as unconditional love, the instant we turn in our hearts and minds to God. *That* is the turning point; that is when ego-transcendence truly begins and the glory of God starts to be revealed to us. As Jesus said, "The first and great commandment is to love God with all your heart and soul and mind." That is the way to seek the kingdom of God.

The Essence of Higher Consciousness

The essence of higher consciousness is never casting anyone out of your heart—to love as God loves. As Jesus said, the second great commandment is to love your neighbor as yourself. When we love as God loves—unconditionally—we are beyond the reach of those who are unloving. We may receive injury from them and we may feel pain— conspirators don't hesitate in that regard—but we are incapable of being hurt or offended in spirit, and therefore are always happy under all circumstances, even in the face of monstrous ill will, injustice and even death. For this reason, love is the greatest "revenge" we can seek against enemies and those who treat us spitefully and wrongly. Is that not precisely what Jesus taught? And is that not precisely how Jesus taught it—by preaching a sermon with his life, as well as his lips?

There will never be a better world until there are better people in it, and the means for attaining that condition—for "building better people"—are democratically available to everyone through the process of growth to higher consciousness. The metanoia process, when completed, results in the state of awareness which Jesus himself had when he said, "I and the Father are one."

That is what Jesus taught and demonstrated—cosmic consciousness, the Christic state of mind, the peace which passeth understanding. That is the human potential—the potential for growth to godhood. That human *potential* is what can change the human *condition* and redeem the world from the hell on earth created by the colossal self-centeredness of our would-be slavemasters.

So, rather than saying that Jesus was the Christ, it is more accurate to say: the Christ was Jesus. That allows for *other* Christs—you and me.

The significance of Jesus, therefore, is not as a vehicle of salvation but as a model of perfection. That is why the proper attitude toward him is one of reverence, not worship. Jesus showed us the way to a higher state of being and called upon us to realize it, to make it real, actual—individually and as the race. This is the true meaning of being born again—dying to the past and the old sense of self through a change of consciousness. To enter the Kingdom we must die and be born again, we must become as a little child. From the perspective of metanoia, the meaning of Jesus' injunction is clear. To re-enter the state of innocence which infants exhibit, we do not merely regress to an infantile level, forsaking our mature faculties. Instead, we *pro*gress through transcendence of the illusion of ego and all its false values, attitudes and habits. We attain a guileless state of mind without giving up the positive qualities of adulthood. We grow into what is called "the higher innocence." We optimize, rather than maximize, childhood, becoming childlike, not childish. Superficial values and capriciousness are simply outgrown, so that we function in the service of a transcendent purpose, rather than seeking self-glorification and power. We discover that heaven and hell are not remote places; they are states of consciousness. Heaven is union with God, hell is separation from God, and the difference is measured not in miles but in surrender of ego and self-centeredness.

There is no way to enter the Kingdom except to ascend in consciousness to that unconditional love for all creation which Jesus demonstrated. That is what the Christian tradition—and, indeed, every true religion—is all about: a system of teachings, both theory and practice, about growth to higher consciousness. But each of us is required to take personal responsibility for following Jesus on that way. That is the key to the Kingdom. Self-transcendence requires honesty, commitment and spiritual practice to cultivate self-awareness. The result of such discipline is personal, validating experience of the fact that systematic alteration of consciousness can lead to a radical transformation of consciousness, traditionally called enlightenment. But this, by and large, has been lost to the understanding of contemporary christendom. Instead, Jesus and the Bible are idolized, and heaven is said to be located somewhere in outer space. Awareness of inner space—of consciousness and the need to cultivate it—is sadly lacking.

So long as people believe in an unbridgeable gulf between themselves and that which Jesus demonstrated, Christianity will not have accomplished its mission. So long as the focus of attention remains on a naive, romanticized image of the historical person Jesus as the King of Heaven rather than on his transpersonal Christic demonstration of how to bridge the gulf between God and humanity, Christianity will not have carried out its founder's intent. "Building bridges"—that should be the main thrust of Christianity. Interestingly, this is explicitly acknowledged in the Roman Catholic tradition whose supreme authority, the Pope, is technically termed the Pontifex Maximus, which is Latin for "supreme bridgemaker." (Again, however, the keepers of this tradition have not retained understanding of that which they keep.)

From Orthonoia to Metanoia through Paranoia

To summarize: In the course of consciousness transformation, there are stages of growth which can be presented in a simple formulation: *from orthonoia to metanoia through paranoia.*

Orthonoia is the common, everyday state of egocentric mind, as in orthodox or conventional. It is the state of consciousness seen in ordinary people, whether they're store clerks, soldiers or senators, policemen, painters or presidents. It's not inherently bad; it's simply undeveloped. It's where we start the process of ascent in consciousness to metanoia. And we arrive there only by going through paranoia.

What is paranoia? Para = outside of, noia = mind. Paranoia is a state outside normal waking consciousness. However, normal means the ordinary egocentric mind of orthonoia in which everything seems fixed, stable and certain. Paranoia, then, is a state in which the mind is *de*-ranged (i.e., taken apart or broken down into components or fragments) and then *re-ar*-ranged through spiritual disciplines into a new and stable configuration so that a clear perception of reality can be experienced without the distorting filter of ego. In the paranoid state of mind, reality is totally uncertain and shifting. The ego is breaking down but the higher-order state of metanoia has not been attained. Confusion, suspicion, fear and suffering are the primary qualities of the paranoid state; demons and mind monsters abound. Because of that, conventional western psychologies regard paranoia as a pathological breakdown, a dysfunction. It often is, of course, but seen from the perspective of metanoia, it is not necessarily always so. Rather, it can be breakthrough—not the final breakthrough, to be sure, but a necessary stage of development on the way to realizing the Kingdom, the New/Aquarian Age.

Paranoia is a condition well-understood by mystical and sacred traditions. The disciplines which people practice under the guidance of a guru or master or spiritual director are designed to ease the passage through paranoia so that the practitioner doesn't get lost in the labyrinth of inner space and become a casualty.

Because metanoia has, by and large, not been experienced by the founders of western psychology and psychotherapy, paranoia has not been fully understood in our culture. It is seen as an aberrated dead end rather than a necessary precondition to higher consciousness. It is not understood that the confusion, discomfort and suffering experienced in paranoia are due largely to the destruction of an illusion called ego. The less we cling to that illusion, the less we suffer.

The world's great spiritual systems, however, understand the psychology of this situation very well and have developed procedures for curing it by disburdening people of their false self-image, their false ego-based identity. It is no accident that society's models of the ideal human being include many saints and holy people. These self-transcendent, God-realized individuals have been revered for many reasons: their compassion, devotion and serenity, their inspirational words of wisdom, their virtuous service to the world. What has been their motivation? Each of them, in his own way arising from his particular tradition or culture, has discovered the secret of the ages, the truth of the saying, "Let go and let God." When the ego-sense is dissolved, when a sense of the infinite and eternal replaces our usual narrow self-centeredness with all its passing, unsatisfying fantasies, there is no longer a mental basis for fear, hatred, anxiety, anger, attachment, desire. Instead, the perfectly harmonious functioning of the cosmos operates through us—and the cosmos is always in balance, always at peace with itself.

A Call to Become Cosmically Conscious

The Christian message is essentially a call to be universal—a call to become cosmically conscious. It is not a fundamentalist warning to beware of false gods but a transcendentalist urging to *be aware* of True God. It is a call to place the Divine at the center of ourselves, not through blind faith but through insightful awareness, not through rigid adherence to ritual and dogma but through graceful expression of cosmic principles. It is a call to recognize God as the transcendent creator of all things, the immanent self of all things and the omnipresent matrix from which all things arise. This is the true meaning of the trinity—the three principal aspects of God and the three primary modes of God-realization: the transcendent Father, the immanent Son and the omnipresent Holy Spirit. (Not so incidentally, the Holy Spirit is the feminine aspect of God—see "The Meaning of the Trinity" in *The Meeting of Science and Spirit*.)

Today the world stands critically close to global holocaust. But a problem cannot be solved at the level of consciousness which generated it. The solution can only be found at a higher level, through transcendence. The answer to our global emergency is emergence. That is, the solution to the problem of history will not be found within history, i.e., within the state of consciousness which generates time, temptation and trouble: ego. The only way out of history into the kingdom of heaven, the only way out of our precarious world situation into a New Age, an Aquarian Age, is a change of consciousness, a transcendence of the false sense of self from which all destructive human behavior arises, including all those darn conspiracies! Only metanoia can provide the means whereby reality is seen clearly and an enlightened global culture is possible. And that is precisely what the Son of Man showed us.

But if the Son of Man showed us the way to that higher state of being, so have other enlightened teachers of humanity shown us the same beckoning evolutionary advance. I do not mean to present Jesus as the sole path to cosmic consciousness. That would be further debasement of his teaching and therefore contrary to the spirit of the New/Aquarian Age. We have been taught by Buddha and Krishna, Lao Tsu and Moses, Mohammed, Zoroaster, Mahavira, Quetzalcoatl, Guru Nanak—founders of the world's great religions. The human race has been guided by many other evolutionary forerunners of a new Earth and a new humanity who have given us the world's sacred traditions, spiritual paths, esoteric psychologies, metaphysical philosophies, hermetic disciplines and genuine occult mystery schools. They have differed in emphasis and cultural orientation, but the core truth of them all is the same: "Thou shalt evolve to a higher state of being and ultimately return to the godhead which is your very self, your ever-present Divine Condition prior to all conditions, names and forms."

Salvation *as liberation or enlightenment* is possible for us at every moment. This is what our spiritual teachers and sages and saviors have told us throughout history, and the unanimity of their voices transcends any sect or religion or organization. Buddhism, for example, has no concept of sin or God, so many Christians feel it is antagonistic to their beliefs. But from the point of view of metanoia, Buddhism and Christianity are reconciled because Buddhism, which does recognize there is wrongdoing in the world, says that it arises in people because they have become separated from their True-self, their Buddha-mind—the higher mind which is known in enlightenment. The Buddha-mind and the Christic mind are one and the same.

If Planet Earth should end up as just a nuclear flash in the sky or a polluted pile of rubble, from the cosmic point of view it will be the loss of just one life-bearing planet circling a minor star in a middle-sized galaxy among billions of galaxies—just an evolutionary experiment which failed. There are probably billions of other worlds, exobiologists tell us, where the evolution of intelligent life forms is going on, with many of them well beyond our own state of development. That termination of Earth can happen, but it need not. The source of our being is calling to us through innumerable forms and channels—through nature and through enlightened teachers—calling us to awaken to our true identity and carry that knowledge forward in the emergence of a higher form of life, a new structure of human society, a new social and political order characterized by God-centered consciousness.

That selfless, compassionate service, that behavioral expression of enlightenment is the key to avoiding global catastrophe and to transforming, rather than destroying, the Earth. Each of us must become our own messiah and thereby redeem the world from sinfulness. Imagine if everyone but those darn New World Order conspirators were enlightened. It would be like the answer to the child's innocent question to her mother: "Mommy, what if they gave a war and nobody came?"

The Kingdom is already among us as the source of our being. To the extent that it is realized in consciousness by people, it is being manifested. The way to God-realization or messiahship or the Kingdom of Heaven is through an ascent in consciousness to that unconditional love for all creation which Jesus demonstrated. In that regard, I'm sure Jesus the Christ would be in perfect agreement with Gautama the Buddha, who taught his followers to work out their own salvation by steadfastly seeking truth. For, as Jesus said, "the truth shall set you free."

Nothing less than that will bring the New Age or Aquarian Age. The real meaning of that Age is a renewing of our minds and hearts through awakening to the presence of God, not simply within us but among us (in other people) and around us (as nature), as well as above us and prior to us—as the All and Only Reality. Only that—only enlightenment or union with God—will transform the world and produce a new humanity.

Enlightenment is possible for you now. That's what spiritual growth is all about. Spirituality is the process of realizing God in every aspect of your life. That means transcending ego and surrendering yourself to the Divine Presence, so that you can say "I am God" with no sense of separate identity, with full recognition that everyone else is God also, and with loving expression of that in your day-to-day existence.

And it will stop those darn conspiracies cold.

CHAPTER 14

ADVICE TO A YOUNG MAN AFRAID OF DEATH

This 1989 letter was a response to a 21-year-old college student who wrote to me in a desperate state. He expressed an "unshakable fear of death and absence of God" which left him "totally miserable and confused" because all his ideas about God, life and the universe were in profound doubt. I've identified him only by the first letter in his name to preserve his privacy and I've expanded the text for this book.

Dear W:

I'm responding to your letter while vacationing with my family. So if this seems disjointed, it's because I'm using spare moments during family activities and driving. It's now 8 a.m. and I'm sitting beside the placid water of Lake Saranac in upstate New York. Ducks are swimming nearby; the mist on the lake is clearing; the trees and grass are drying from the morning dew. Altogether, it is a scene which a Zen master might capture in a haiku poem. In a few vivid words, the Zen master would draw a verbal image which addresses all the philosophical and psychological issues you're struggling with, and he would offer, cryptically, an answer which perfectly resolves them. The Zen tradition, like all sacred traditions, emphasizes *direct experience* and holds out the promise that, through personal effort, the practitioner can attain a state of consciousness which transcends all limitations of time and space, matter and causality, yet which, paradoxically, includes them all in perfect integration, so that there is no conflict or contradiction or doubt in the practitioner's mind about the cosmic "all-rightness" of mortal limitations, loss and death. Heaven and Earth embrace. Time and eternity unite. Individuality and loss of personal identity are completely reconciled. And love shines unceasingly amid it all. I have directly realized this, beyond all intellectual concepts and dogma.

However, *my* experience is not the answer to *your* dilemma. It is only my strong assurance to you that there *is* an answer. I can tell you *about* the answer, but the truth itself, which is the answer, must be discovered and realized by you personally. It will be a terribly painful process because ego-transcendence—which is one name for the answer—is *always* painful. But it is absolutely necessary if you want to know the truth which can set you free. There is no way around it, yet with determination and sincerity of purpose, you will learn the age-old wisdom which answers all your questions and leaves you infinitely satisfied, infinitely assured, infinitely beyond fear, regret and the suffering of problematic life-situations. Everything will be transformed for you, even though your circumstances remain the same. The horror, the emptiness, the absurdity of existence which you describe will vanish as you see their illusory nature arising from your own mind—not from the cosmos but from your misperception of the cosmos. Although I am not an existentialist, I appreciate the wisdom of Jean-Paul Sartre's declaration: "Life begins on the other side of despair."

* * * *

It's the next day. I'm sitting in a hotel lobby, after having a continental breakfast. My family is still asleep. I'm an early riser so this is a good time to continue my response:

At 21—your age—my sense of tragedy and mortality was almost totally overwhelming. My college studies at Dartmouth, where I was an English major, brought me to a state in which my existence seemed utterly absurd. Death hung over everything. As I walked the streets, I could, and did, visualize people I saw as if they were ancient, with their skulls visible beneath their facial skin. I wasn't trying to do that; it just spontaneously happened. I'd been immersed in study of religion, philosophy, psychology and science, but none of it provided satisfactory answers to my urgent questions of who I was, why I was here, what it means to be aware of being aware, i.e., self-conscious. I was searching desperately for meaning which had ultimate significance in the face of those issues which are likewise assaulting your awareness. Like Buddha some 2,500 years earlier, the reality of sickness, old age and death confronted me, undermining all the comfortable illusions I had about the course of my life. The received answers I'd absorbed from my family and my culture could not stand up to the harsh examination I was forced to give them. Though I'd been raised in the Episcopal Church, the answers given/learned in catechism seemed ridiculously shallow and juvenile. Nothing made sense except love. I was desperate for something which might anchor me in the rush of confusing life-events. Only love seemed to offer hope and comfort. I was on the verge of breakdown—or so it seemed. In retrospect, I can say it was all grace which led me to such a state of psychological compression, in preparation, not for breakdown, but for breakthrough. However, that was still several years away. I still needed to clear away much mental conditioning and illusion so that unblurred perception of reality might happen.

God Was Nowhere Present

When I was your age, though, my situation was very much like yours. God was nowhere present; death undermined all my glorious dreams; and the masses of humanity seemed to be living superficial, trivial and robotic lives. Even heroic efforts were eventually undermined, it seemed. Civilization was a sham—or at least no more than a futile gesture at holding back the cold night of eternity. Humanity was alone in a hostile universe.

I was attending college on an NROTC scholarship, which meant I was to serve as a naval officer for four years after graduation. I'd gone into my military training with vague but romantic dreams of glory, but as my search for meaning deepened, I had to question it all—the notion of patriotism, military might, combat and killing another human being, giving my own life for a national policy which seemed only to mask gross greed and exploitation of other nations and cultures by the military-industrial complex, etc. Shortly after I got into naval service, it became obvious that my deepest instincts and attitudes were not suitable for military responsibilities. Again, my world-view was assaulted and shattered. I was mixed up and hurting; in fact, in the deeper aspects of my life, I was a mess. So one day, in profound confusion and anguish, I took out my .45 pistol and put it to my head, intending to commit suicide as a way out of my suffering.

Obviously I didn't kill myself, and I'll tell you why as a way of responding to your letter. What I'll tell you now is not simply a recollection. It's intended to show you the way out of your own suffering.

Parapsychology as a Breakthrough to Reality

During my senior year of college, as I browsed in the library, I found a book which really excited me. It was called *The Reach of the Mind* by Dr. Joseph B. Rhine, the "father" of parapsychology. As a youngster, I'd always been drawn to ponder human capabilities, especially powers of the mind. However, until I got to college, my explorations were undirected and ungrounded. Mostly they consisted of reading science fiction and fantasy. With my discovery of parapsychology, however, I found a perspective and a credible discipline—science—for examining the nature of mind and self without the inherent barriers which the implicit atheistic materialism of conventional science brings to such examinations.

All along I was searching for myself, and parapsychology suggested there is an aspect of human experience which transcends time, space and death. So from that moment of discovery during my senior year, I had a thread to follow which seemed to lead toward a way out of the confusing labyrinth of questions and doubts plaguing me. As I read parapsychological literature and began to correspond with parapsychologists, I could see a *rational* basis for *religious* faith in an afterlife. Parapsychology suggests that mind extends beyond the body and beyond an individual's lifetime. It converges with elements of spiritual creeds in all sacred traditions.

That was a deeply refreshing discovery, although it didn't have all-consuming importance for me in the maelstrom of life-issues I was dealing with, not the least of which was marriage, our first child and my obligation as a naval officer to strap on my .45 and lead boarding parties onto Soviet ships during the Cuban Blockade, if that should come to pass. No newlywed young father could be happy in those circumstances; at least, I couldn't.

A Suicidal Moment

Well, I didn't have to lead a boarding party after all because the Soviet ships turned back before reaching the line of no return. But my psychological situation nevertheless remained near overload. I was training as a nuclear weapons officer and all my humanitarian instincts and values recoiled from that. As I look back on myself then, I see strong signs of clinical depression. But that medical condition wasn't recognized then and, even if I'd had a name for my state of mind, I felt I couldn't talk to anyone about it. The cause wasn't biochemical; it was spiritual. I was searching for meaning, but finding none, just as you are now.

Looking back, I can see that I was intuitively employing two of the great mystical practices for self-realization. First, I was meditating on death—not in a formal, disciplined way, but nevertheless in a profoundly contemplative and sincere way. (Sincerity of effort can often make up for lack of formal training.) Death threatened all meaning in my life. Second, I was asking myself, in a most intense and steadfast manner, the koan-question "Who am I?" I wanted to know myself at rock-bottom reality, beyond all my roles and socially defined identities.

My later experience and consciousness research showed me that both are practices which a variety of sacred traditions, including Zen and that of the twentieth century Indian sage Ramana Maharshi, recommend for attaining clarity and peace of mind. At the time, however, I didn't understand myself to be doing either. I was simply trying desperately to find a way out of my anguish and suffering. But I didn't seem to be making any headway. Or more precisely, I didn't seem to be making any heartway. I was sick at heart, sick to the core of my being, as far as I could understand myself.

So one day, in profound confusion, I put my gun to my head, contemplating what that might accomplish. I didn't want to go on living in such mental anguish, but as I pondered my perplexity while recalling the data from psychic research, it seemed a pretty good bet that if I pulled the trigger, I'd just "wake up dead" in a postmortem state where my problems would still exist because they were in my own mind—my own indestructible consciousness. In addition to that, I abhorred the idea of leaving my young daughter with the stigma of a suicide father. Last of all, the pure joy of watching her grow up—the innocence and wonder of it all—was something I didn't want to miss. That, too, suggested something ultimately meaningful in an otherwise bleak, absurd existence—something beyond the hell of my isolated self, something with an aura of self-transcendence.

So I put my gun away and decided to live, even though in huge pain. In my free time after carrying out my military duties, I continued feverishly delving into psychology, parapsychology and mysticism, seeing more and more clearly that my received worldview and its subtle but powerful ramifications were quite inauthentic—just a psychological conditioning I'd undergone in the process of acculturation. I saw that others had become truly free and that there were methods for attaining that. I desired that strongly.

A Mystical Moment

About six months later, by an act of grace, a spontaneous mystical experience occurred to me and a radical realization of my inherent divinity-immortality showed me the truth of what I'd dimly understood intellectually, conceptually. It was a classic mystical experience: the total loss of ego-boundary and isolated self-sense. I went from "God is nowhere" to "God is now here." I went from alone to all-one. The cosmos became me, even though I retained individuality. All notion of ultimate separation was transcended, so that what had previously seemed *division* was understood as *differentiation*: unity-in-diversity, the One-in-all. I realized the presence of God, without intellectual filters. It profoundly reoriented my life and brought me a sense of heaven-on-earth. It showed me possibilities for higher human development—my own and the world's.

That certainly was not the end of my "unlearning" process, but I think I've said enough to show you that I say with utter conviction that you are in a somewhat similar position to realize directly what I'm telling you about indirectly. You are in the blessed state of readiness which most of humanity is ignorant of. You are in an evolutionarily advanced condition, about to make a quantum leap in consciousness. The point is this: there can be no ego-transcendence until there is first an ego. The process of growing up has inevitably led you to form an ego. Now you're ready to go beyond that state of consciousness. The suffering and disillusionment you're going through are necessary preparation to undermine the ego and allow your consciousness to function in its original, free, natural state, which is beyond ego. ³ In that state, all which is necessary for your happiness and understanding is given, is eternally present. That is the case right now, even though you don't see it. However, with that radical change in consciousness, with that new sense of self, with that unshakeable knowledge which answers the ultimate question "Who am I?", you will find that your questions/criticisms about God, death, society, love, etc., will be answered in a way which allows you to discern the real from the unreal and the true from the false in all aspects of your life, from church to family, from local citizenship to international affairs, from work to play, from relationships to worship.

Choose to Live—and Learn

All that is necessary for you to begin the process is to decide to *live* in search of truth. When the student is ready, the teacher appears. As Jesus said, ""If you ask for bread, you will not be given stones." A benevolent universe has been nourishing you for growth to a higher state of being, and will continue to do so. That is what life is all about. You're just waking up to the fact, but you've been divinely favored to be nudged awake at so young an age. Don't ignore the gift by falling into complacence about your human potential to unfold spiritually. And bear in mind that the degree of suffering you experience is a *direct measurement* of the amount of ego you have invested in the situation. If you can bring yourself to pray, simply address God as whatever you conceive the highest good to be. Surrender your self-centeredness to that highest good with the words "Thy will be done; show me the way." Study the lives of saints and enlightened teachers. Let your search include research, i.e., read books such as Ken Wilber's *No Boundary*, Alan Watts' *Psychotherapy East and West*,[2] Lex Hixon's *Coming Home*, Aldous Huxley's *The Perennial Philosophy*, Huston Smith's *Forgotten Truth* and my anthology *What Is Enlightenment?* Read the sacred scriptures of world religions. Join organizations such as the Academy for Spiritual and Consciousness Studies,[3] the Association for Research and Enlightenment,[4] a bible study group and a meditation group or prayer group. Above all, be patient amid your efforts: all will happen as the time is right for you. You can't take heaven by storm.

---

[2] Alan Watts holds an especially warm spot in my heart because his book *Psychotherapy East and West* affected me powerfully and positively when I read it at age 22, shortly before I contemplated suicide. It was the first book of his which I read. Alan declared in clear prose that my suffering was due to the illusion of ego. Although I didn't understand his message experientially—that would come a year or so later via the mystical experience I mentioned—it nevertheless provided an intellectual reorientation toward a way out of my confusion and personal hell. Thereafter, I avidly devoured his writings and in 1964, as my ship was preparing for combat in Vietnam, I wrote to him to express my gratitude for the spiritual lifeline he'd provided to someone whom he never knew. I said that I was going into war—such was the understanding aboard my ship—and if I didn't survive, I would nevertheless die with an appreciation for his wise and helpful words.

To my surprise, he replied with a brief note on a card; it touched me deeply that he should be so caring about an unknown correspondent among the many letters he constantly received. As I mentioned in "Enlightenment and the Martial Arts" in *The Meeting of Science and Spirit*, it provided a moment of sanity in the seemingly crazy world of military operations at that time. Alan and I corresponded occasionally thereafter, and in February of 1974, when I was working at The Institute of Noetic Sciences in Palo Alto, California, he and I planned to meet at the Esalen Institute in Big Sur, where we were scheduled to give separate seminars. The week before, however, he died of a heart attack, so I never got to meet him. Nevertheless, he lives on for me in the mighty work he initiated as one of the founders, so to speak, of the consciousness revolution now transforming world affairs. I regard him as one of the sages of the Second Axial Age now occurring.

[3] Academy for Spiritual and Consciousness Studies, P.O. Box 84, Loxahatchee, FL 33470 USA. Website address: www.ascsi.org

[4] Association for Research and Enlightenment, P.O. Box 595, Virginia Beach, VA 23451.

Someday in the not-too-distant future, you will smile with infinite delight at your present circumstances. For now, grit your teeth and hold on and think of Longfellow's adage, "The lowest ebb is the turn of the tide." To which I add the folk-wisdom saying, "The longest way 'round' is the shortest way home."

With best regards,
John

P.S. I've just re-read your letter and feel I should speak briefly to your anthropomorphic conception of God. You have an image of God as the gray beard in the sky, like Michelangelo's painting of "The Creation" in the Sistine Chapel. But that image in your mind is simply an immature, juvenile conception, useful and appropriate for instructing children, yet far from reality. Atheists, such as Freud and Nietzsche, declare there is no god. They are right in the sense that God is not a gray beard in the sky. It's time for you to move beyond that. You are attributing qualities to God which are not there. God doesn't enjoy our suffering. God doesn't cause our pain. God is not a cruel, sadistic father. All too often people project onto the heavens what they themselves are or have experienced, and call that divinity. But it's not divinity—it's childish nonsense and misunderstanding.

The more you know yourself, the more you know God. The deepest center of the self—called the *atman* in Hindu thought—is also the deepest center of the cosmos—called *Brahman*, the godhead in Hinduism. In other words, the Creator and the created are essentially one; you are a manifestation of God. So as you go evermore deeply into inner space, you are simultaneously probing outer space— through consciousness. Consciousness is the meeting ground for inner and outer reality. Consciousness is the mystery to be understood. *Mysticism* is the means of "going within" or "going below" superficial religious concepts to know God directly, beyond all childish images and adolescent formulations of doctrine. *Metaphysics* is the means of "going without" or "going above" to understand the structure of the cosmos and the nature of reality. Ultimately, the two converge and are united in the experience of realizing God. So to know God, you must "unlearn" much, let go of childish notions, and let God reveal himself/itself as reality.

Reflect on this: You think you are a human having a spiritual experience, but in reality you are Spirit having a human experience.[5] Why do you assume you are apart from God right now? That is a false assumption. You are never apart from God. How can you or anyone ever possibly be apart from God, the source of all creation and the center of your very existence? If God is omnipresent, and God is in all things, and God is the very center of your being and the basis of your existence, then what are you doing right now which prevents you from recognizing that and living in accordance with it? Look within yourself and answer that question. The "answer" will identify precisely what is going on in your consciousness which creates the illusion of separate self, moment to moment to moment. See through that illusion. When you lose an illusion, when you are disillusioned, what have you lost? Only a trick of the mind, only a misperception, a misunderstanding. That is another way of saying you have lost nothing but rather, paradoxically, have gained a clear(er) perception of Reality. An old Zen saying applies here: "Now that my house has burned down, I have a better view of the sky."

P.P.S. At the risk of numbing you by my long-windedness, W, I want to offer some thoughts about your suffering. The problem of suffering is addressed by all the major religions. Buddhism is especially clear and penetrating in this regard, but I don't know of any which do not see suffering as part of the spiritual path. However, their understanding of the how and why varies, even within a single tradition, depending upon whether the one offering an explanation is a fundamentalist, rationalist or mystic. In Christianity, for example, some fundamentalists describe suffering as God's wrath and judgment visited upon us for sin. Mystics, however, tend to say—and it has been repeated often—that suffering is the "first grace."

What accounts for the different interpretation of the same event? As the rishis of ancient India said, *knowledge is structured in consciousness.* The fundamentalist sees things through ego-driven consciousness. Hence, his world view is narrow and rigid; it emphasizes childish dependence and authoritarian control: There is sin, there is suffering, and because the Bible tells me so, that's the end of the story.

---

[5] W was a Roman Catholic. Recently a friend pointed out the following in the *Catechism of the Catholic Church*, which I would have shared with W if I'd known of it at the time.

However, the mystic, Christian or otherwise, says there is more to the story. The mystic says that suffering is directly proportional to the amount of ego operating in us. Sin is essentially the ego in operation, so in that sense, the fundamentalist is right: suffering is the wages of sin. But the larger picture is this: Sin means literally "missing the mark", i.e., the target. God is the target, so when we "aim" for God and through spiritual practice hit the mark, our sinfulness is diminished, our willful self-centeredness and egocentricity is reduced. Through the process, our suffering is reduced. The person who has transcended the illusion of ego or separate selfhood has no suffering; he or she is totally centered in God. That's not to say there's no pain, no physical discomfort, no difficult circumstances or troubling events for the mystic. There can be and often are, but it is not taken personally by the mystic and does not disturb his or her sense of the presence of God as God operates lawfully through all the levels of the cosmos. From the mystic's perspective, suffering is self-inflicted through the free-willfulness by which we insist on being in the world but unaligned with God.

Suffering is the first grace because it is the way the cosmos operates to awaken us to our nonalignment and disharmony when nothing else seems to do the job. People go to church, hear a sermon or homily, but all too often they don't take it seriously or internalize it or contemplate it and apply it to their lives. So they have ears but hear not, they have eyes but see not. They think they can take a couple of laps around the rosary and the sin-slate is wiped clean. But reality doesn't work that way.

Understood from the mystic's point of view, suffering is a gift, a grace, excruciating as it may be in the moment of experiencing it, as you are now. It's not that God *wants* us to suffer. Quite the opposite; God wants us to be happy, to share his felicity (*ananda* in the Hindu and Buddhist traditions). To do that, we have to make choices, and the stupid ones lead to suffering. We have free will. We can ignore red lights, we can run through stop signs. But eventually that train is going to pass through the railroad crossing just as we're recklessly trying to speed through it, and then there's suffering. That doesn't mean God is vindictive or wrathful. It simply means there are lawful operations running the cosmos, including ourselves. Blessedly, we have the means to recognize and understand the operation, and then conduct ourselves accordingly. When we do, *voila*—no suffering. We are released into the freedom and unconditional love and felicity of God. And then we can smile in wonder at the absolute perfection of the universe, in every aspect of its operation, including all that suffering, even as we work with compassionate objectivity to help awaken suffering people to the fact that they are causing it to themselves.

P.P.P.S. For the record, I'm not a member of any religion or denomination. In the spirit of ecumenism, I honor them all but belong to none. I feel that wearing a religious or denominational label tends to separate me from people who wear different labels and value them more than open, honest relations, so I consciously "choose to have none so that I may be one" with all others. I can call God by any of the thousand names which religions use because Truth is one.

Three of my grandparents were Jews; they were born culturally Jewish but grew up nonobservant of Judaism. Two of them—my father's parents—gravitated to Unitarianism and one of them, my mother's father, converted to Christianity later in life. His wife was a Christian Scientist. I was raised as an Episcopalian by my mother; my father was an agnostic with no religious affiliation except his childhood Unitarianism.

I'm grateful for the religious training I received because it helped me to understand the difference between Christianity and churchianity. Churchianity is egoic misunderstanding of Jesus's teaching and egoic misdirection of the organizational power and structure supporting what is actually a sacred tradition for God-realization. Churchianity has been the source of so much folly and brutality in history. I'm sure Jesus would be appalled at many things which have been done in his name but which were pure sectarianism. So I don't call myself Christian any longer, in order not to wear a label which divides me from people of other faiths. I'm not a Christian but I am trying to be Christed, and I belong to the same religion as God does. As I see it, Buddha didn't teach Buddhism and Jesus didn't teach Christianity. They both taught paths to enlightenment and couldn't have cared less about a name for their paths. That, not anything denominational, is what matters to me.

There is a big difference between superficial religion and deep spirituality. I have a spiritual agenda, not a religious one. I say that because your letter expresses religious doubts. If institutional religion were truly the embodiment of what is meant by the word *religion*, "spiritual" and "religious" would be synonymous. (As a minister friend of mine humorously put it, "For God's sake, don't be religious!") The word *religion* comes from the Latin *re ligare*, meaning "to tie again" or "to bind back." The tying or binding is back to God. Religion, in its ideal form, is a theory and practice for God-realization. In that sense, I have a religious agenda, but only in that sense. I have no wish to belong to any particular religious institution. God is on no one's side (which is the same as saying God is on everyone's side), but clearly there are people who seek to live God-based lives and those who couldn't care less. There are also institutions which seek to structure societal conditions to better support and nurture the process of God-realization. Insofar as a religion or other institution does that, by whatever name or from whatever culture, I advocate and endorse it, but only that. And that is the approach I urge you to take in your search for self-understanding. I have no wish to undermine anyone's faith—only to deepen their understanding and appreciation of their faith to the point of seeing it as a path to enlightenment.

Note: Several years later W wrote to me in a much happier frame of mind. He thanked me, saying that his "sense of spiritual confusion" had disappeared. He enclosed a copy of the letter above to remind me of what I'd said to him, which is why I am able to reproduce it here and add footnotes.

WHY DID THE WORD BECOME FLESH?

...to make us "partakers of the divine nature" (2 Peter 1:4)... "so that man, by entering into communion with the Word and thus receiving divine sonship, might become a son of God" (St. Ireneaus.). "For the Son of God became man so that we might become God" (St. Athanaseus). "The only-begotten Son of God, wanting to make us sharers in his divinity, assumed our nature so that he, made man, might make us gods" (St. Thomas Aquinas).

CHAPTER 15

WHAT IS KUNDALINI?

The awakening of kundalini. Chakras. The kundalini experience. These terms are heard more and more often in connection with the experience of people questing for enlightenment. A large number of commentators have offered a variety of explanations and discussions of the terms. However, there is not complete agreement, and frequently there is strong disagreement on just what they mean. Coming from the Indian spiritual tradition, the words are alluring but mysterious. There is a mystique about them which, for many people, prevents clear understanding—and therefore usefulness—in their efforts to grow, to unfold, to advance along the spiritual path.

Over several decades of spiritual research and consciousness studies, I've investigated the subject and tried to cut through the "Himalayan fog" to get to the truth about kundalini. Here's how I see the situation.

Kundalini is a Sanskrit word meaning "coiled up" like a snake or a spring. Traditionally called "shakti" or "the serpent power," kundalini is symbolized in ancient Hindu, Vedic and Tantric texts as a sleeping or resting serpent coiled at the base of the human spine. The image implies latent power or untapped potential to expand or rise up, like an awakened snake or a wound-up spring which can uncoil suddenly with great strength. In modern terms, kundalini refers to the human potential for spiritual growth and higher human development which can be activated by various physical and mental disciplines, including yoga.

Kundalini shakti flows upward from its resting place at the base of the cerebrospinal column, it is traditionally said. As it does so, it passes through a number of chakras or energy centers. The number varies from five to ten or even more, according to various traditions, but the most common number is seven. They are located from the coccyx to the crown of the head, and are symbolized as multi-petaled flowers. When the kundalini shakti flows through them, the chakras are activated and the flower petals symbolically open into a full bloom.

Different human capacities and faculties are also associated with the chakras, and when they are activated, the capacities and faculties are awakened or greatly enhanced. The crown chakra is associated with enlightenment. Thus, if the process of awakening kundalini is completed, the result is an enlightened person recognizable by the many superior qualities and abilities he or she demonstrates.

Although the word kundalini comes from the yogic tradition, nearly all the world's major religions, spiritual paths and genuine occult traditions see something akin to the kundalini experience as having significance in the process of a person's growth in God-realization to a higher state of being. (Genuine occultism aims at personal transformation and self-transcendence; degenerate or incomplete occultism aims at psychic experiences or magical powers.) The word may not appear in the traditions, but the concept is there nevertheless, wearing a different name or symbol, yet recognizable as a key to attaining godlike stature. It has been described in the ancient records of Tibet, Egypt, Sumer, China, Greece and other cultures and traditions, including early Judaism and Christianity. The Pharaoh's headdress, the feathered serpent of Mexico and South America, the dragon of oriental mythology, the serpent in the Garden of Eden—all are indicative of kundalini. So is the caduceus—the twin snakes coiled around a staff—symbolic of medical practitioners. The symbol is said to be derived from the god Hermes, founder of the hermetic tradition of higher knowledge.

Nor is the concept limited to indicating the growth potential of an individual. Considered from the viewpoint of personal transformation, kundalini is said to be a path to enlightenment. However, if a large number of enlightened people were to appear in society at the same time, the result could well transform society itself. The kundalini experience, then, in the broadest sense, is evolutionary—a path for the advancement of the entire human race to a higher state. The concept embraces the species; it symbolically depicts our capacity to grow and ascend from our primitive animal origins to a condition which is truly transhuman and godlike.

The kundalini concept, then, is a sort of map or cartography of evolution and enlightenment, albeit in obscure language and veiled allusion. It marks the transformational journey which must be undertaken individually but which, if sufficient numbers of individuals successfully complete, can result in societal, planetary transformation and, eventually, a higher form of humanity.

Thus, kundalini presents a radical idea which goes to the roots of important social trends involving spiritual seeking and religious awakening. Just as important, in the view of some scholars and scientists, it has significance for a number of related aspects of unfolding human mentality: genius, creativity, intellectual and artistic talent, insanity, psychic powers, sociopathic behavior. Last of all, it is a powerful idea for explaining in a unified way many of the mysteries of the biological, physical and social sciences. The kundalini concept in its essence is a comprehensive theory of human nature—a concept which holds that humanity has a tremendous potential to unfold, develop, grow, evolve to a higher state.

Anything so profound is not going to be definable in a single term or image. The answer to the question "What is kundalini?" has many levels, ranging from the physical to the metaphysical, from the personal to the transpersonal. It is as vast as the cosmos itself but as individual as our own hopes and aspirations for discovering the answer to the mystery of life and the riddle of existence.

APPENDIXES

APPENDIX I

BOOK REVIEW OF
THE ROOTS OF CONSCIOUSNESS

This appendix reviews *The Roots of Consciousness* by psychologist Jeffrey Mishlove (Random House, 1975). It was published in *New Age Journal* (November 1997).

Bad news and good news. First the bad: the book is overpriced. This could have been avoided by eliminating 16 pages of full-color photos which boosted costs by at least several dollars. The photos, ranging from Kirlian photography and firewalking to chakras and UFOs, are most familiar to readers in the psychic, paranormal and occult fields, so little would have been lost.

More bad news: the book is misnamed. Psychic phenomena and psychic abilities are a *fruit*, not a root, of consciousness (and not always a sweet fruit either!). A full century of psychic research has made it clear that psychic phenomena are never going to be understandable unless we get to *their* roots in the mystery of consciousness itself.

Therefore the book's subtitle, "Psychic Liberation through History, Science and Experience," is misleading. Liberation comes from the realm of spirit which is, depending on your metaphor, higher or deeper than the merely psychic. The psychic is not the mystic—period. The psychic is mystifying, not enlightening, and has value as a tool for liberation only if the seeker recognizes that and moves *through* the psychic to a higher or deeper level. Otherwise he'll be trapped in the spell, the glamor, the endless fascination of myriad phenomena which lead him in circles, going nowhere—and especially not into self-knowledge.

But now for the good news: Mishlove knows that and points it out in the text. So having disposed of what I consider to be a major philosophic error in the book, albeit a catchy title, I'm ready to give credit where credit is due.

The Roots of Consciousness has three major sections. The first, "History of the Exploration of Consciousness," is the weakest. It is a once-over-lightly which surveys major traditions leading up to 20th Century psychic research. You find lots of interesting topics here: the ancient Egyptian description of the soul leaving the body, the Eleusinian mysteries, Christian and Arabian explorations into consciousness, consciousness in the Age of Reason. But this section tries to do too much and should have been a volume in itself, at least. (Yoga and Tibetan Buddhism, for example, are covered in four pages.)

The second part, "Scientific Approaches to Consciousness," gets us into the mainstream of psychic research, and does it well. The text takes a sort of catalogue approach to psi, supported by useful quotes from various appropriate texts. You'll meet some superpsychics such as Uri Geller and Nina Kulagina, you'll walk on fire, attend seances, have out-of-body experiences, learn psychic healing, and watch over the shoulder of laboratory researchers such as J. B. Rhine and Stanley Krippner as they perform their milestone investigations. Those investigations, however, are important in scientifically establishing the actuality of psi, *not* in explaining how it works—which we still don't understand after one hundred years of research.

That brings us to the last section, "People, Places and Theories." Here I was genuinely delighted to meet the Reflexive Universe theory of my friend Arthur Young, investor and founder of the Institute for the Study of consciousness in Berkley. Young's work is not widely known, but ought to be because he is a brilliant and original thinker. In this section also is an atomic physicist, Jack Sarfatti, who is attempting to integrate psychic phenomena and quantum mechanics. Then we jump to practical applications of psychic abilities in dowsing, education, crime detection, business, medicine, and so on—psi in the modern world. A short listing of various organizations in the psychic, occult and spiritual fields wraps up the whole package.

There are some serious shortcomings in *The Roots of Consciousness* because it is overly ambitious, but that kind of failing is nevertheless creditable, as is Mishlove's writing style which makes for easy reading. And most certainly *not* among the shortcomings are the graphics and layout, which are well done throughout. The book is amply illustrated, as befits the kind of encyclopedic approach it takes. And the artwork in front and back by Vijali, along with her cover painting, are major highlights in the book—a trip in themselves.

APPENDIX 2

BOOK REVIEW OF *THE EYE OF SPIRIT*

This appendix reviews *The Eye of Spirit—An Integral Vision for a World Gone Slightly Mad* by Integral psychologist-philosopher, Ken Wilber, (Shambhala Publications, 1996). It was published in Noetic Sciences Review (Spring 1997.).

First, a disclaimer: I am a long-time fan of Ken Wilber's work. I helped get his first book, *The Spectrum of Consciousness*, published and described him as "The Einstein of consciousness research" because his breakthrough insights integrated the four forces of psychology (behaviorism, psychoanalysis, humanistic and transpersonal) in the same breathtaking way Einstein's did for the four forces of physics. Wilber elaborated and refined his perspective, quickly becoming pre-eminent in the fields of noetics and transpersonal psychology, and extending his reach into many other areas of science and culture. What was first termed spectrum psychology is now called integral psychology to denote Wilber's elegant integration of psychology with all fields of knowledge.

The Eye of Spirit reinforces the pre-eminence of Wilber's map of reality. Readers will find more of his stunning formulations, incisive analyses and sage pronouncements on various issues, ranging from feminism, art and literary theory to Retro-Romanticism, the evolution of culture, and the relation between God and political agendas. Wilber's lithe, engaging prose often rises to moments of poetic beauty. The final chapter on the nature of enlightenment—from which the book's title is drawn—is so eloquent that it becomes the literary equivalent of a Zen master's stick with which meditators are powerfully struck to induce satori.

One example (of many which could be given) of Wilber's surgical expertise: In "Born Again," an essay on Dr. Stan Grof's noetic research, Wilber exposes a pre/trans fallacy in Grof's key concept of "perinatal." He identifies a contradictory double meaning in it and charges that "with this hidden, dual definition...Grof has rather completely confused chronology with ontology." It is not necessary to re-live clinical birth in order to enter the transpersonal, Wilber demonstrates. But he also clarifies what is true and valuable about Grof's data.

For all its brilliance, there is nevertheless a gap in Wilber's work. I refer to paranormal phenomena, the topic with which the Institute of Noetic Sciences began, using psychics such as Uri Geller and Ingo Swann as laboratory subjects. The research sought to understand how their extraordinary powers of mind originate and operate, how those powers can be trained, how they can be applied to planetary problems.

The answers were far from clear then, and remain so. Likewise, integral psychology has little to say about what the West calls psychic abilities or psi and the East calls siddhis. It acknowledges they exist, but their emergence, development and control receive little commentary. Furthermore, the energy or energies involved in psychic phenomena are not well described by integral psychology (or by science, numerous theories notwithstanding, possibly excepting Thomas Bearden's). Wilber doesn't give us the insightful understanding which allows prediction of dynamics and voluntary control of such energies as he does transformations of consciousness. His model of human development is sheer genius for the way it lays out mental growth from infancy to enlightenment—except for the psychic aspect. It's not that the model is wrong; it's simply incomplete as a description of mind.

That's not a criticism, though, because no one else has such a predictive model. Wilber does usefully point out in an earlier book, *Eye to Eye*, that in psychic events, the mind and senses are not vertically transcended, but simply horizontally extended. That is in keeping with wisdom traditions, which warn that psychic development is not the same as spiritual growth.

But is psychic development a necessary stage on the spiritual path or an aberration? Is it, a la Michael Murphy's perspective (in *The Future of the Body*), an emerging evolutionary change or, as J. B. Rhine saw it, an atrophied holdover? What is the relation, if any, between character development and, say, psychic healing, telepathic ability, mediumship or clairvoyance? Why have some sages lacked significant psychic ability? Why have some superpsychics lacked significant ego transcendence? The answers have not been given in any scientifically useful way by either the sages or the psychics, nor has parapsychology discovered satisfactory answers. So it is understandable that Wilber remains largely silent about these questions. More research is needed. Meanwhile, integral psychology remains, for me, the best guide to self and societal unfoldment, and *The Eye of Spirit* refines it even more.

ABOUT THE AUTHOR

JOHN WHITE is an author and educator in the fields of consciousness research and higher human development. He has been Director of Education for The Institute of Noetic Sciences, a research organization founded by Apollo 14 astronaut, Edgar Mitchell, to study human potential for personal and planetary transformation, and President of Alpha Logics, a school for self-directed growth in body, mind and spirit.

Mr. White has published 18 books, including *America, Freedom and Enlightenment: An Open Letter to Americans about Patriotism and Global Society, The Meeting of Science and Spirit, A Practical Guide to Death and Dying, The Gulf of Tonkin Events—Fifty Years Later, The UFO Experience—From Alien Abductions to Zeta Reticuli* and the forthcoming books *Enlightenment 101: A Guide to God-Realization and Higher Human Culture* and *The Pledge of Allegiance & The Star-Spangled Banner: A Patriot's Primer on the American Spirit.* He has also edited anthologies, including *The Highest State of Consciousness, Psychic Exploration, Kundalini, Evolution and Enlightenment* and *What Is Enlightenment?*

His writing has appeared in *Reader's Digest, The New York Times, The Wall Street Journal, Esquire, Woman's Day, Omni* and other publications. His books have been translated into ten languages.

As a lecturer and seminar leader, Mr. White has appeared at colleges, universities and spiritual/human potential centers throughout the U.S. and Canada, and before public and professional organizations such as Esalen Institute, Spiritual Frontiers Fellowship, Interface, Oasis, Human Dimensions Institute, American Anthropological Association,

Academy of Religion and Psychical Research, American Orthopsychiatric Association, Theosophical Society and the International Congress of Meditation and Yoga. He has also made radio and TV appearances throughout this country and Canada.

Mr. White was born in 1939. He holds a Bachelor of Arts degree from Dartmouth College (1961) and a Master of Arts in teaching from Yale University (1969).

A Vietnam War veteran, he attended college on an NROTC scholarship and then served four years as a naval officer, primarily in antisubmarine warfare and nuclear weapons. He and his wife, Barbara, have been married for more than fifty years. They have four children and seven grandchildren, and live in Cheshire, Connecticut, USA.

Paperbacks also available from
White Crow Books

Elsa Barker—*Letters from a Living Dead Man*
ISBN 978-1-907355-83-7

Elsa Barker—*War Letters from
the Living Dead Man*
ISBN 978-1-907355-85-1

Elsa Barker—*Last Letters from
the Living Dead Man*
ISBN 978-1-907355-87-5

Richard Maurice Bucke—
Cosmic Consciousness
ISBN 978-1-907355-10-3

Stafford Betty—
The Imprisoned Splendor
ISBN 978-1-907661-98-3

Stafford Betty—
*Heaven and Hell Unveiled: Updates
from the World of Spirit.*
ISBN 978-1-910121-30-6

Ineke Koedam—
*In the Light of Death: Experiences on
the threshold between life and death*
ISBN 978-1-910121-48-1

Arthur Conan Doyle with Simon Parke—
Conversations with Arthur Conan Doyle
ISBN 978-1-907355-80-6

Meister Eckhart with Simon Parke—
Conversations with Meister Eckhart
ISBN 978-1-907355-18-9

D. D. Home—*Incidents in my Life Part 1*
ISBN 978-1-907355-15-8

Mme. Dunglas Home; edited, with an
Introduction, by Sir Arthur Conan
Doyle—*D. D. Home: His Life and Mission*
ISBN 978-1-907355-16-5

Edward C. Randall—
Frontiers of the Afterlife
ISBN 978-1-907355-30-1

Rebecca Ruter Springer—
Intra Muros: My Dream of Heaven
ISBN 978-1-907355-11-0

Leo Tolstoy, edited by Simon
Parke—*Forbidden Words*
ISBN 978-1-907355-00-4

Erlendur Haraldsson and
Loftur Gissurarson—
*Indridi Indridason: The Icelandic
Physical Medium*
ISBN 978-1-910121-50-4

Goerge E. Moss—
*Earth's Cosmic Ascendancy: Spirit
and Extraterrestrials Guide us
through Times of Change*
ISBN 978-1-910121-28-3

Steven T. Parsons and Callum E. Cooper—
Paracoustics: Sound & the Paranormal
ISBN 978-1-910121-32-0

L. C. Danby—
*The Certainty of Eternity: The Story
of Australia's Greatest Medium*
ISBN 978-1-910121-34-4

Madelaine Lawrence —
*The Death View Revolution: A
Guide to Transpersonal Experiences
Surrounding Death*
ISBN 978-1-910121-37-5

Zofia Weaver—
*Other Realities?: The enigma of
Franek Kluski's mediumship*
ISBN 978-1-910121-39-9

Roy L. Hill—
*Psychology and the Near-Death
Experience: Searching for God*
ISBN 978-1-910121-42-9

Tricia. J. Robertson —
*"Things You Can do When You're Dead!: True
Accounts of After Death Communication"*
ISBN 978-1-908733-60-3

Tricia. J. Robertson —
*More Things you Can do When You're
Dead: What Can You Truly Believe?*
ISBN 978-1-910121-44-3

Jody Long—
*God's Fingerprints: Impressions
of Near-Death Experiences*
ISBN 978-1-910121-05-4

Leo Tolstoy with Simon Parke—
Conversations with Tolstoy
ISBN 978-1-907355-25-7

Howard Williams with an Introduction by Leo Tolstoy—*The Ethics of Diet: An Anthology of Vegetarian Thought*
ISBN 978-1-907355-21-9

Vincent Van Gogh with Simon Parke—*Conversations with Van Gogh*
ISBN 978-1-907355-95-0

Wolfgang Amadeus Mozart with Simon Parke—*Conversations with Mozart*
ISBN 978-1-907661-38-9

Jesus of Nazareth with Simon Parke—*Conversations with Jesus of Nazareth*
ISBN 978-1-907661-41-9

Thomas à Kempis with Simon Parke—*The Imitation of Christ*
ISBN 978-1-907661-58-7

Julian of Norwich with Simon Parke—*Revelations of Divine Love*
ISBN 978-1-907661-88-4

Allan Kardec—*The Spirits Book*
ISBN 978-1-907355-98-1

Allan Kardec—*The Book on Mediums*
ISBN 978-1-907661-75-4

Emanuel Swedenborg—*Heaven and Hell*
ISBN 978-1-907661-55-6

P.D. Ouspensky—*Tertium Organum: The Third Canon of Thought*
ISBN 978-1-907661-47-1

Dwight Goddard—*A Buddhist Bible*
ISBN 978-1-907661-44-0

Michael Tymn—*The Afterlife Revealed*
ISBN 978-1-970661-90-7

Michael Tymn—*Transcending the Titanic: Beyond Death's Door*
ISBN 978-1-908733-02-3

Guy L. Playfair—*If This Be Magic*
ISBN 978-1-907661-84-6

Guy L. Playfair—*The Flying Cow*
ISBN 978-1-907661-94-5

Guy L. Playfair — *This House is Haunted: The True Story of the Enfield Poltergeist*
ISBN 978-1-907661-78-5

Carl Wickland, M.D.—*Thirty Years Among the Dead*
ISBN 978-1-907661-72-3

John E. Mack—*Passport to the Cosmos*
ISBN 978-1-907661-81-5

Peter & Elizabeth Fenwick—*The Truth in the Light*
ISBN 978-1-908733-08-5

Erlendur Haraldsson— *Modern Miracles*
ISBN 978-1-908733-25-2

Erlendur Haraldsson— *At the Hour of Death*
ISBN 978-1-908733-27-6

Erlendur Haraldsson—*The Departed Among the Living*
ISBN 978-1-908733-29-0

Brian Inglis—*Science and Parascience*
ISBN 978-1-908733-18-4

Brian Inglis—*Natural and Supernatural: A History of the Paranormal*
ISBN 978-1-908733-20-7

Ernest Holmes—*The Science of Mind*
ISBN 978-1-908733-10-8

Victor & Wendy Zammit —*A Lawyer Presents the Evidence For the Afterlife*
ISBN 978-1-908733-22-1

Casper S. Yost—*Patience Worth: A Psychic Mystery*
ISBN 978-1-908733-06-1

William Usborne Moore—*Glimpses of the Next State*
ISBN 978-1-907661-01-3

William Usborne Moore—*The Voices*
ISBN 978-1-908733-04-7

John W. White—*The Highest State of Consciousness*
ISBN 978-1-908733-31-3

Lord Dowding—*Many Mansions*
ISBN 978-1-910121-07-8

Paul Pearsall, Ph.D. — *Super Joy*
ISBN 978-1-908733-16-0

All titles available as eBooks, and selected titles available in Hardback and Audiobook formats from www.whitecrowbooks.com

Printed in September 2023
by Rotomail Italia S.p.A., Vignate (MI) - Italy